# A Practical Guide to Arts-related Res

# A Practical Guide to Arts-related Research

**Maggi Savin-Baden**
*Coventry University, UK*

and

**Katherine Wimpenny**
*Coventry University, UK*

SENSE PUBLISHERS
ROTTERDAM/BOSTON/TAIPEI

A C.I.P. record for this book is available from the Library of Congress.

ISBN: 978-94-6209-813-8 (paperback)
ISBN: 978-94-6209-814-5 (hardback)
ISBN: 978-94-6209-815-2 (e-book)

Published by: Sense Publishers,
P.O. Box 21858,
3001 AW Rotterdam,
The Netherlands
https://www.sensepublishers.com/

Printed on acid-free paper

For our supportive husbands John and Steve and our patient children
Anna, Zak, Thomas, Harry and Elliot

# TABLE OF CONTENTS

# ACKNOWLEDGEMENTS

We wish to thank all those artists, researchers and practitioners from around the globe who have added their contributions to this book, which makes it a much richer text than our voices alone. Our thanks are also due to John Savin-Baden for proof reading the text and Gemma Tombs for checking and formatting it. Any mistakes are thus our own.

Our revels now are ended. These our actors,
As I foretold you, were all spirits and
Are melted into air, into thin air:
And, like the baseless fabric of this vision,
The cloud-capp'd towers, the gorgeous palaces,
The solemn temples, the great globe itself,
Ye all which it inherit, shall dissolve
And, like this insubstantial pageant faded,
Leave not a rack behind. We are such stuff
As dreams are made on, and our little life
Is rounded with a sleep

Shakespeare (1610) *The Tempest Act 1V Scene 1*

# INTRODUCTION

This book emerged out of our interest in, and encounters with, those working in arts-related fields wanting to undertake research in a variety of ways. As researchers our stories both overlap and collide with arts-related research and it was the troublesomeness and challenge of such intersections that prompted us to write this book. At the same time, our stories and researcher lives also sit at the interstices of inquiry-based learning, arts-informed research and more traditional forms of qualitative inquiry:

*Maggi:* My interest in research methodology stemmed from teaching a research methods course at Glasgow University in the early 1990s, just after a number of new textbooks had been published. As a lecturer, the challenge I faced was working with Master's students who were undertaking collaborative and participatory research in areas of poverty, homelessness and low literacy, and yet the texts available provided little practical guidance or help. As a result I spent many years studying what was on offer and trying to make it inspiring and useful, particularly for first year students who hated learning about research. Today, having been a researcher for over 25 years, I tend to use the most appropriate methodology for the issues I am studying, but I remain convinced that qualitative studies needed to be positioned and located properly in terms of methodology and philosophy. My interest in arts-related research began through colleagues in medicine in the late 1990s. More recently I was asked to evaluate an arts-based intervention for older people that was being introduced by our local theatre in Coventry, UK. This evaluation was the catalyst for exploring how I might use arts-related research to evaluate an arts-based intervention. As I devised the evaluation and read around the subject, it became apparent that there are many examples of arts-related research, but relatively little philosophical positioning, methodological stance or guidance on how to undertake it in practice. Although I realised that those in the arts focus strongly on process and the creation of the work, and perhaps more importantly do not wish to be pinned down and boxed in, what did seem to me to be important was that they could argue their position in rigorous ways. For me this has been the focus of this text, to provide clear arguments and rigorous places to stand for those undertaking arts-related research. Yet I have been concerned that leading edge researchers and artists continue to struggle to have their work valued. Researchers such as Harrison, Leggo and Weaver Hightower, all mentioned in this text, have found that the rigours of expectation and academic life have often stood in the way of their creativity, which seems to me to be creating spaces of confusion and injustice in arts-related research.

*Katherine:* Having worked as an occupational therapist for 10 years in health followed by 10 years as a lecturer and now as a research fellow in higher education, my interest in arts-related research has arisen from multiple layers of experience, not least through my own creative practice and insights from arts processes that have informed my belief, following Reilly (1962), in how the use of our hands, mind and will can influence our health and creatively can deploy our thinking, feeling and purposes.

I have a particular interest in participatory and collaborative approaches within qualitative inquiry whereby learning with co-participants is reciprocal, where participants are not kept at a distance and where perspectives and viewpoints can be explored through the research process to address, question and promote issues about, for example, social justice and citizenship. I have realised how the written word alone restricts what can be known and shared about a phenomena, especially when as the researcher I have appreciated the complexity of data gathered. Using the arts and the artistic process has enlivened my research practice and enabled me to enrich, deepen and expand the ways in which I explore, question and open up conversations with research participants, whilst also leaving space for the viewer to add to the picture, which sits well when considering the complexity of human life and experience. For me this text has provided opportunity to further explore and share my enthusiasm and practice in conducting robust arts-related research and importantly to provide support to other researchers considering its use.

As two women writers, both with husbands and children, who work full time, as well as run, cook and create, we seek to make our values as researchers evident. We share common ground in terms of valuing the importance of researcher stance, reflexivity, diversity of meaning and ways to celebrate diverse means of expression.

This text will outline the principles and practices of arts-related inquiry and provide both suggestions about conducting research in the field as well as case study examples. The ideas presented here have emerged from our own experiences of undertaking arts-related research and the challenges of implementing these approaches with little guidance. The book therefore draws on personal research, practice and experience. This book also addresses the concerns academics increasingly appear to be voicing, about developing the scholarship and practice of arts-related research. There is a need for greater attention to, and clarity on, issues of theoretical positioning, methodology and methods when conducting robust and reputable art-related research, which this book undertakes. Through this book we will therefore argue that arts-related inquiry:

- Is a rich, creative, exciting, yet complex field of inquiry which requires greater consideration of the art / research / researcher and researched relationships than it has done to date.
- Is an area that requires further depth and detail to support those new to the field of inquiry in questioning theoretical and methodological fits, and adopting the most appropriate methods.
- Requires greater consideration of the process and products of inquiry, including issues of analysis, interpretation and representation of arts-informed inquiry, and the extent to which it lends itself to collaborative inquiry.

# ARTS-RELATED RESEARCH

## INTRODUCTION

This chapter will explore the concept and practice of arts-related research and provides a typology to explain this. Although we suggest a number of different types here, arts-related research remains difficult to define because it takes distinct forms and is used in diverse contexts. What makes arts-related research both challenging and interesting is that it is not prescriptive, and invariably the rubrics that generally inform qualitative inquiry are not applied easily. This chapter locates arts-related research, positions it philosophically and then situates it in terms of its core values, as well as exploring the idea of the artistic process. The second section of the chapter provides a table of types and then details each one.

## LOCATING ARTS-RELATED RESEARCH

Arts-related research is defined here as research that uses the arts, in the broadest sense, to explore, understand and represent human action and experience. It has emerged as a concept and practice from the interaction between art and social science. Early studies began with artist-researchers using and following their creative process as their research method. The result was that arts-related research developed through the relationships early artists/researchers had with their own creative processes, and their beliefs that letting research and creativity unfold together would cause both art and research to emerge as outcomes. Although the focus of this approach began with the artistic process, arts-related research has changed and developed into a number of different forms, which we define and explain below. The typologies we present here as forms of arts-related research use media to provoke questions in audiences, for example, by taking a stance on a social issue and/or political concern. The researcher therefore uses media both to create artefacts, and to use them as a means of understanding and examining the experiences of the participants and researchers involved in the arts-based research. The idea in this kind of research is to create, examine and interpret art in ways that illustrate both the artistic process and the impact of arts and issues on peoples' lives. Thus arts-related research focuses on both the end point and final representation, as well as on the process and expression of the work in a context. However, as researchers we suggest that there are central values that cross all the typologies of arts-related research presented in this chapter, and to explain this we draw on the earlier work by Savin-Baden and Major (2013):

*Table 1.1. Principles of arts-related research*

*The research is guided by a moral commitment* — For researchers in this field the work produced is expected to, as it were, "take a stand." Research and the related artefacts may, and often do, present and promote personal transformation both for the artist-researcher and the viewer.

*Knowledge is generated through the work* — It is not always initially clear to the artist / researcher in what ways knowledge might be generated. It might be in terms of what the work evokes for others or it might present a socio cultural change to those who encounter the work. At other times knowledge might be generated by the artist / researcher for themselves through the work they are creating.

*There is a strong focus on reflexivity* — In arts-based research, because of its very nature, the presence of the artist is evident through the work. However, because of the nature of arts-based disciplines and the critical and complex nature of art itself, the sense of reflexivity is heightened compared with other research approaches. Heightened reflexivity is not just a characteristic of this form of inquiry, but is central to it, since arts-based research takes a critical stance towards itself and the world around. Therefore for most arts-based researchers, the moral stance and sense of interruption through art is central to the research

*Accessibility is a firm focal point* — A central stance in arts-based research is that the work does not only have the potential to challenge and transform but also that it is available and accessible to a wide and diverse audience. Such accessibility means not just that an audience can see or read the work but also that they can understand, engage and relate to it.

*Diverse forms of quality are celebrated and brought together* — Quality is difficult to define and manage in relation to arts-based research, particularly as some artist researchers in this field suggest that the overarching purpose is knowledge advancement through the work that matters, rather than the work itself. Others suggest that good art is also good research. However, the art, as used, must support the research goals, whilst its quality, in terms of aesthetics, must hold meaning. Yet at the same time there also needs to be a quality of coherence which reflects the relationship between the purpose of the research and the means of undertaking it.

*There is a sense of authenticity* — The work and research must be intertwined and mutually shaping so there is sense of integrity about the art and the research. This is perhaps the most central feature of arts-based research, which is related to the idea of trustworthiness or plausibility in other forms of qualitative inquiry. This aspect is essential so that there is consistency and rigour characterizing the relationship between the research and the artwork.

(Savin-Baden & Major, 2013:292-293)

However, we also suggest that in terms of philosophical and methodological positioning arts-related research sits within and across post-modernism, constructionism and constructivism. These are defined below and referred to further in Table 1.2.

## Post-modernism

This is used to describe the post-modern condition, or belief systems characteristic of the post-modern era. The post-modern condition is characterised by a shift in attitude and position within humanity (as suggested by Foucault (1979) and Nicholson (1990)), which ultimately has led to movements such as feminism and racial equality movements. Post-modernism and post-structuralism are often treated as interchangeable terms. While there is overlap, post-modernists take a stance towards the state of the world; the period following the modernist period, whereas post-structuralists explicitly seek to deconstruct structures and systems that are seen to normalise people and ignore subtext. Foucault and Barthes may be claimed by either camp, and indeed both often are.

## Constructionism

Social constructionists argue that, instead of focusing on the mind (the cognitive approach), it is important to recognise that the world is shared. The argument is that the world is produced and understood through interchanges between people and shared objects and activities, so that hidden or private phenomena such as emotions gain their meaning through social settings and practice, and are therefore socially constructed. Thus reality is not entirely external and independent of individual conceptions of the world, and therefore signs and systems play an important part in the social construction of reality as individuals make and experience meaning together. Social constructionist research involves a focus on deconstruction, dialogue, negotiation and reconstruction, with the goal being to understand shared and co-constructed realities.

## Constructivism

Constructivism is based upon the notion that reality is a product of one's own creation. Constructivists doing research seek to understand the way meanings are constructed and to capture how such meanings are presented and used through language and action. They use a range of approaches to seek individuals' reconstructions of their realities, and might use data collection methods such as interviews, narratives and new or existing artefacts that express individuals' ideas and experiences.

3

## UNDERSTANDING TYPES OF ARTS-RELATED RESEARCH

This section outlines the variety of arts-related research available, and begins by explaining arts-based pedagogy, as there is often a confusion between this and arts-related research. However, it is important to understand too the importance of the artistic process which has been debated widely over many years. Many artists and researchers suggest that the artistic process is something that blends the relationship with the medium with emotion and the pursuit of quality. Liebman (2009) suggests that the artistic process requires the artist to express some comment or view about life through their work, while seeking to engage with areas such as philosophy and history in order to inform and guide their emotions when creating. He also argues for stages of the process, summarized below, which include:

1. Absorption of principles and techniques that are seen as standard in the field and the ability to present these to a given standard.
2. Personalization, whereby the artist personalizes past and contemporary styles
3. Innovation, where the artist contributes something unique to the field
4. Further study of technique and past achievements in the field to broaden the artist's work in order that a wider range of emotions and ideas can be conveyed.

It is clear that the artistic process is difficult to define and pin point because the resonance between artist and process is private and not easy to articulate. The use of contemplation and observation for many people are seen as starting points in the process. This is followed by a sense of needing to organize the materials and medium, as well as the way the work might begin, followed by reflection on the process and perseverance with it. However, arts-related research takes many forms and it is evident that in this field not everyone undertaking arts-related research is a designated artist. There are others who may not be artists *per se* yet do use creative practices in their works, such as arts therapists, occupational therapists and historians. Table 1.2 below provides an overview of arts-related approaches:

*Arts-inquiring Pedagogy (Including Practice-based Research)*

Arts-inquiring pedagogy is the use of inquiry within the teaching of art, of whatever sort, to ensure that students develop critical abilities in the class room. This is very similar to approaches such as problem-based learning where the starting point for learning is a problem, challenge or issue, which guides the students to seek out what it is that they do not know in order to solve or manage the problem set. The main focus of arts-inquiring pedagogy is on inquiry for learning, which comprises the following characteristics:

– Prompts students to question and critique rather than focus on attaining a 'right answer'
– Students work to identify learning gaps
– Students gain new information through practice-based inquiry
– Staff act as challengers and discussants

Table 1.2. Overview of arts-related approaches

| Type | Definition | Key features | Focus | Commonly adapted paradigms | Related theorists |
|---|---|---|---|---|---|
| Arts-inquiring pedagogy | Using arts to teach inquiry and enable learning to occur through exploration and inquiry | Centralising the artistic process, criticality and inquiry are central learning processes | Use of inquiry for learning | Critical awareness/ developmental learning theorists | Dewey, Mezirow, Rogers |
| Arts-based inquiry | Artistic process is used by artists, researchers and participants in order to understand the art itself or understand a phenomenon through the artistic process | Use of arts for personal exploration of a particular concern or issue | Artistic process | Postmodernism Post structuralism Constructivism | McNiff (2008) |
| Arts-informed inquiry | • Where art is used to represent the findings of a study • Where art is used to represent a response to the findings of an issue or situation studied | Use of art to enhance understanding, reach multiple audiences and make findings accessible | Issues of representation | Postmodernism Post structuralism Constructivism | Saldana (2010) |
| Arts-informing inquiry | Art is used in order to evoke a response from an audience (in the broadest sense) made to a situation or issue; the response may or may not be captured. | Making meaning through complex performances/ products that have power and are evocative. | Issues of response | Constructivism/ Constructionism | Herman (2005) |
| Arts-engaging inquiry | The use of art to engage communities/marginalized groups | Community engagement and provoking change | Change and transformation | Constructivism/ Constructionism | Mezirow, Freire, hooks |
| Arts-related evaluation | The use of the artistic process to undertake, represent and disseminate evaluation. | Creative processes central to understanding an issue through evaluation | Evaluation of and through the artistic process | Constructivism/ Constructionism | Simons & McCormack (2007) Snowber & Cancienne (2003) |

Arts-inquiring pedagogy focuses on higher order thinking in the context of exploring challenges and issues. It is also often used to describe a form of learning where the students decide on their own questions and queries during the artistic process and the making of the work, so that they both inquire and learn at the same time.

This approach is often referred to as practice-based research and whilst it invariably sounds as if it is research-led, in the main it tends not to be. Practice-led research focusses on understanding and advancing knowledge about practice. This form of research uses practice as the central component of the methods adopted and does have some similarities with action research. Invariably the results of these kinds of practice-based studies result in the emergence of new knowledge that has both operational and practical significance for the area of practice being researched. Haseman and Mafe (2009) identify the following conditions which characterize the practice-led research process and have been summarized below:

*The problem of the research problem* — There may be a need to delay the identification of the research question as the practice unfolds. The research problem may only be identified in the final phase of the research process.

*Repurposing methods of research language* — Articulating a research methodology or methods may not always serve the research purpose well due to the problem of trying to 'map' the artistic process, techniques, nuances and directions of the work within a traditional discourse of research. Instead, the techniques of practice need to be repurposed into the language and methods of research. Thus the artist/ researcher's thinking is not discipline specific but exists as part of a wider research process which needs to stand up to methodological scrutiny and research outputs. What can occur then is a more familiar habitat in which practice-led researchers can contribute to the wider research field and believe their contributions to be valued.

*Research context is all* — Before critical significance of a practice-led research project can be identified, the relevant research context must be clearly identified in order for findings to begin to be understood and claimed.

*The relevance of 'professional frames'* — The professional framing of the research is required to reveal the impact of the practice. Professional frames play a key role in knowledge definition, for example in terms of ownership and what can be considered legitimate.

*Forms of reporting* — Issues of representation, the materiality of the research, the reading of that content are all important considerations to report as is the translation from one to the other form.

*Deliberating on emerging aspirations* — The research aims are broad and may include aspirations that relate to politics, justice and aesthetics.

*Arts-based Inquiry*

Arts-based inquiry is the use of the artistic process; the making and doing of art as a means of understanding experience. In this form of inquiry, for example, dance might be used to understand more about specific aspects of dance or a particular issue connected with dance such as choreography. Arts-based inquiry in this instance not only involves the artist (of which ever type) but also those who are involved in the art work in some way, including the participant and possible other researchers. Thus researchers and participants use art for personal exploration to make sense of the problem or medium, so that the research and the artistic process overlap. In practice the artist-researcher might bring together short plays created by different individuals. However, at the outset a protocol needs to be developed both about what is to be included and how the context will be used to evoke a response. McNiff (2008) suggests that it is helpful to create a clear method that can be described and then implemented in a straight-forward way and also can be replicated by other researchers. Further, he believes that despite being complex and difficult, it is essential to try to convey arts-based inquiry to others through text in order to reach a wide audience. Thus arts-based inquiry focuses on both the end point and final representation, as well as the process and expression of the work in a context.

*Arts-informed Inquiry*

Arts-informed inquiry focuses on the use of arts to inform the ways in which the research is undertaken. In the main we argue that it comprises two types: as a means of representing findings and as a means of representing a response to the situation being studied.

---

Arts-informed inquiry comprises two types:

a. Where art is used by artists and researchers to represent the findings of a study
b. Where art is used by artists and researchers to represent a response to a situation studied

---

Arts-informed inquiry is perhaps one of the most well-known forms of arts-based research and comprises the process of using art to illustrate and represent findings. For example, Walker in the 1980s (Schratz & Walker, 1995) argued that pictures should not be used instead of words, but as a way for prompting discussion about the nature of context. More recently photo story and digital story telling have been used as a means of bringing together visual narratives, through the use of arts and images to represent narratives. Digital story telling involves asking participants to present their point of view using images. It requires them to consider the use of their voice, the choice of music and the way the story is paced and presented. Thus overlap occurs between arts-informed research and narrative inquiry.

Many artist-researchers began using these new ways of representation by including narratives, poetry and photographs in traditional journal articles (for example, Park-Fuller 2003). More recently, exhibitions have been used to represent findings, as have virtual worlds and virtual reality. For example, Harrison (2013) created a circus tent. He argued:

> As an Artist-in-Residence in a Toronto District School Board high school I began my research. This involved setting up an open door studio through which students could come and go ongoing through the process of the research. An autoethnographic, arts informed project was begun in which I would explore the narratives of my own life as a lens into growing up gay in rural Ontario in the 1960s and 1970s. The dissemination of the findings was achieved through painting on the walls of a small circus or freak show tent. Images on the outside of the tent were appropriated from Ringling and Barnum Bailey's circus and freak show advertisements and historical photographs (Jando et al, 2008) intertwined with self-portrait images of the more negative ways I am imagined as a gay man. On the inside walls of the tent autoethnographic images were painted which explore the formative years of my life and how I imagined myself. The painted freak show tent is the dissertation. An artist's catalogue was created documenting the studio, the research conducted to produce the narratives, the creation of the tent and the tent itself. It became the document that with the tent itself could be defended to conclude my doctoral research, for it both documented and contextualized the cultural artifact (Kahle & Internet, 1998) of the tent.

What is significant about Harrison's work is that the work is used to enhance understanding, reach multiple audiences and use media to make research findings accessible to a variety of people. A different example is that of Saldana (2010) who uses ethno drama which employs the techniques of theatre production to produce a performance of participants' experiences. He argues:

> In theatre, the term for a play written to be read but not performed is a 'closet drama'. Researchers can certainly compose a field note-based script as a closet ethnodrama, but the next step and true test of a play's effectiveness come from its production mounting on stage. I encourage all researchers not only to develop written scripts, but to explore their realization through a staged reading or performance. (p. 68)

*Arts-informing Inquiry*

This form of inquiry is designed to evoke meaningful thought about art. Thus here art is used to evoke a response to a situation, but the response may or may not be captured. Those in the arena of arts-informing inquiry tend to focus on evoking meaning through the creation of complex, liquid and messy products or performances, ones that are oriented toward an "evocative" epistemology (Denzin, 1997). Here it is possible to see the overlap with performance studies. What Denzin means by an 'evocative' epistemology is that it offers a way of knowing that goes beyond vision, representation and mimicry; so that it is a way of knowing that performs rather than represents the world. This kind of performance creates powerful research spaces and is capable of exerting powerful influence on ways of "doing" research. Yet some of these kinds of evocative epistemologies and forms of inquiry are problematic and almost too messy, and without any kind of text or interpretation the evocative epistemology is easily lost. Perhaps one of the best examples of this is the work of Herman (2005), who recognized that non participants who viewed, heard or encountered evil acts responded to the telling of the stories related to these acts, and that this needed to be captured. She explained:

> I am interested in the images of evil events, in particular the images of genocide, and how they affect nonparticipants in these events. I want to know more about how and what researchers learn from other people's representations of our vast creative capacities for cruelty and what is our experience when we engage these images. How do they affect those of us who were not there? I believe we nonparticipants need to stay creatively engaged with this (fortunately) mediated experience to help prevent its continuing occurrence. (p. 468)

What is significant here is that often the responses to experiences and data are disregarded and we do not recognize the value and importance of such responses. In practice much of this arts-informed research occurs in hidden spaces, such as artists' studios and with community groups at art colleges and centres, and therefore it can be quite difficult to both discover and access this kind of inquiry. However, what is essential is that such research creates more data, additional content beyond what was initially presented and therefore this adds new layers of meaning to studies. This kind of response capturing has been used in a variety of ways. For example, following exhibitions of photographs and stories of holocaust victims, survivors have been asked to retell their stories in response. Similarly, those visiting an exhibition of drawings and paintings of one woman's 30 year story of long term mental illness were asked to share their response to the work later. The power of the presentations of both the holocaust and the mental illness elicited often unexpected responses which in turn became data. A further example of the use of representation is Stellarc, who integrates technology into his body and has suspended himself from his flesh as an installation.

This approach to arts-informed inquiry is not about representing findings per se but about representing a response to the findings. Invariably this kind of arts-based research is captured as parts of a wider project and sometimes the responses are gained informally or through podcasts; therefore in the main they are published less than other forms of arts-related research.

*Arts-engaging Inquiry*

This use of art engages communities, marginalized groups and diverse and different audiences. The focus of this typology is in community engagement and provoking change. It developed from the work of Boal (1979) who created drama theories and concepts entitled The Theater of the Oppressed. Boal (like Freire (1970) who argued that teaching was oppressive) argued against the continued dominance of a privileged few and the use of theatre for political propaganda. Instead he suggested arenas such as Newspaper Theatre where local problems are presented to audiences, and Invisible Theatre, which is used to discuss political activity. The focus here is on interaction between audience and performers, which becomes blurred as the performance evolves, so that the audience become 'spect-actors,' whose roles are seen as being equally important to the performance as those of the actors on stage. Projects that have been inspired by the work of Boal include the Interactive Theatre Project (itp) at the University of Boulder, Colorado, USA, which provides professionally scripted/improvisational performances and facilitates discussions on social issues. The audience members are seen as central to the performance, and scenes are created specifically for the where audience to identify and empathize with all of the characters.

A different example is the work of Upton, who integrates virtual worlds into real spaces in order to gain audience response and interaction. Extract/ Insert for example, was an installation in Second Life and The Herbert Art Gallery, Coventry, UK which took place over a week. (http://vimeo.com/32502129). Upton and colleagues created an environment in which avatars from around the world interacted with visitors to the gallery. Upton's installation attracted over 5,000 visitors and as he explains:

> We succeeded in enabling a physical audience to engage and interact with a global virtual audience within an immersive mixed reality space. Participants were able to socialise and be extracted and inserted into each other's alternative realities... we created an installation 'that inspired participants to consider the nature of space, identity, reality and communication'

Jamieson too has examined the new theatrical form of cyberformance (live performance by remote players using internet technologies) and she suggests that cyberformance offers a means to integrate new technologies and theatre. What is important about this work is that the sense of engagement transcends fixed boundaries, so that face to face and online audiences are valued. There is additionally the recognition of the '*intermedial* audience—a new form of audience existing in-between the online and the proximal, in the liminal time and space of cyberformance' (p. 54). She explains:

> The blurring of disparate time zones by events such as attending the premier of a performance the day before it happens disrupts the certainty of measured time. It may be almost tomorrow, but my audience are still staggering through

today and yesterday. Somebody's got to get up in the middle of their night. Cyberformance exists outside the clock, in a chunk of time shared by all the participants. The shared moment is real time, the venue is a virtual space, and the result is live theatre. (Jamieson, 2008: 56)

## *Arts-related Evaluation*

This form of evaluation uses the artistic process to undertake, represent and disseminate evaluation. In many ways this is a new way of seeing and using evaluation which is strongly holistic, thereby shifting it firmly away from traditional forms of evaluation. As Simons and McCormack argue:

> Artistic knowing in evaluation creates new opportunities for evaluators to express their creativity, for participants to overcome barriers to participation, and for both to advance the sophistication of evaluation practice (Simons & McCormack 2007: 308)

Snowber and Cancienne (2003) used dance not only for evaluation but also to disseminate findings. In this kind of arts-related research the importance of the creative processes are seen as central to facilitating the understanding of an issue by engaging with the whole person. Thus the values implicit in these kinds of evaluations become explicit, through the creative process which in turn enables the evaluator to shape the evaluation. The evaluation then connects with participants as well as shaping the design throughout the life of the evaluation. The analysis and interpretation of data are also seen as a component of the artistic process, so that the movement of different parts of data can be compared with a dance whereby the evaluator examines patterns, feelings and emotions of data in order to interpret them. Dissemination of findings occurs through artistic forms, for example: Wimpenny and Savin-Baden (2013) presented the collation of the participants' responses through an arts-based installation, see Figure 1.1.

However, arts-related evaluation is an approach that is used to examine the value or worth of something and this itself makes such research complex and challenging, whilst also bringing with it the need for clarity and honesty. The fact that any form of evaluation is located in a political context brings with it both a sense of unease and a demand for honesty. This unease emerges because values and morals are explicit and evident in evaluation in ways that are often less obvious in other forms of research. This in turn brings to the fore the centrality of power in evaluation studies, and implicit within any evaluation is the question of judgement. For example, funders often want the evaluated project to be seen as effective and creditable, and may attempt to pressurise the research team to adapt or exaggerate findings. The research team thus need to be clear about its role and stance at the outset of the evaluation, as well as being clear how and with whom the findings will be shared.

*Figure 1.1. Arts-based representation of findings: Beginnings*

Arts-related research is varied and many people find it to be an interesting journey. Finley has been using it since 1998 and shares her reflection below:

---

*Author Reflection*

**Susan Finley**, Washington State University, Vancouver Canada

In many ways, my personal journey as an arts-researcher corresponds with the emergence of the field of arts-related research. Early on, I explored a range of research approaches that drew upon arts and humanities in data collection, analysis, and representation, before settling into *critical* arts-based research. Moreover, I have explored a wide range of art-making techniques in doing and re-presenting research—including, collage (2002), painting (2001), short story (Finley & Finley, 1999), performance (Finley, Cole, Knowles, and Elijah, 2010; Saldana, Finley, and Finley, 2005), and poetry (2000, 2011). Similarly, my 1998 dissertation included collage, as well as a screenplay (republished as a serial in the *Journal of Thought*). My thesis argued the need for new research methodologies, particularly arts-based approaches, as a means to diversify the educational enterprise and break away from a trajectory of repetition without renewal in educational systems. Initially, the major task for arts-based researchers was to establish the legitimacy of its methodologies for researching human experience. My first published article appeared in the inaugural issue of *Qualitative Inquiry (QI)* (Finley & Knowles, 1995). It was an experiment with alternative text-aesthetics as well as a reflection on the epistemology and practice of arts-and-research. Meanwhile, *QI* became the premier venue for publishing arts-research, including a very early, special issue, devoted to developments in arts-based research methods (Finley & Mullen, 2003, Finley, 2003). This history of arts-in-research will again be reviewed in an upcoming, commemorative twentieth anniversary edition of *QI*. Throughout, my primary research focus has been educational equity and access, with particular attention to the experiences of economic poverty and homelessness. This has been realized through research projects with street youth, residents of tent communities, and unhoused children and families, sheltered and unsheltered. Throughout, my practice has been that of artist-as-researcher, researcher-as-artist. What became increasingly clear over the trajectory of my research efforts was that my arts-based approach to doing research was inextricably integrated with the ethics of emancipatory and transformative tenets of critical curriculum theory. Increasingly, this approach has become defined by my involving research participants in doing community arts, such as poetry workshops, mural painting, and performances as forms of self-reflective, action research through the arts.

---

*Continued*

As a critical arts-based researcher, I seek to do research that is deliberately transformative of social structures, and inspires its participants and its audiences to reflection and to ethical, political action (Finley, 2011). Ethically, arts-created in community are the voice of the community and its individuals. Thus, in a special issue of *Cultural Studies-Critical Methodologies* devoted to critical homelessness (Finley & Diversi, 2011) several participants in a five-year poetry workshop with street youth are published under their own authorship. This is an example of using the arts to expand the scope of intellectual autonomy of these poet-artists and to make a political statement about the limited access most of my participants have to any of the systems of knowledge production, including the publication of social research about their own lives. An upcoming special issue of *Cultural Studies-Critical Methodologies* (Finley, 2014) exhibits works from other researchers that explore further the possibilities for critical arts-based inquiry: the pedagogy and performance of a radical ethical aesthetic.

## CONCLUSION

Arts-related research is a methodology that transcends arts and social science in order to reflect diverse human experience. However, as we discuss in later chapters, it is also being used in medicine, health and law. Although we have delineated different types within this chapter there are overlaps between them. We have considered them separately to highlight key differences between them. What is evident is that adopted arts-related approaches tend to result in introducing more questions than answers, both for the researchers and those viewing the findings of the study. What makes it both challenging and interesting is that it is not prescriptive and often the principles of qualitative inquiry cannot be applied easily. However, it is a form of inquiry that perhaps does put political, social and moral issues centre stage in ways that other qualitative approaches do not.

# THE HISTORY AND DEVELOPMENT OF ARTS-RELATED RESEARCH

## INTRODUCTION

Arts-related research has been gaining increasing attention across higher education and the arts. For many researchers the range of arts-related research seems to offer opportunities to interrupt, disrupt, and create space for discussions about dominant discourses in research and practice across a variety of disciplines. Yet at the same time such spaces remain troublesome and contested. This chapter will map the origins of arts-related research in terms of its historical and disciplinary development. It will explore the processes and practices that have informed its development and examine global trends and differences.

## HISTORY AND CRITICAL TURNS

The field of qualitative inquiry has continued to evolve since early twentieth century debates about whether post-positivism was an appropriate paradigm for social research (Savin-Baden & Major, 2013:3). The dominance of positivism on social research (1900 – 1940s) led to researchers objecting to values where knowledge was viewed as reliable and research findings as those which could explain and predict. Post-positivism itself maintains positivistic perspectives, in that reality exists and maybe determined through logical processes (Savin-Baden & Major, 2013). Between 1950 and 1970 new approaches emerged and social scientists began to act on the appreciation that traditional techniques for conducting research were not adequate when answering the many questions to be asked and from diverse perspectives. Yet researchers typically continued to conduct their research using quantitative approaches.

Arguably it was from the 1970s onwards which saw researchers adopting more diverse forms of inquiry, including narrative and hermeneutic approaches that borrowed from other disciplines and were arts based and reflexive (Denzin & Lincoln, 2005). Indeed, Finley (2005) suggests two key issues which created the space for arts-related inquiry to emerge; the first arose through the increasing need for qualitative research to address the interpersonal, political, emotional, moral and ethical relational skills that develop and are shared between the researcher and the researched. Secondly, issues relating to the reporting of research were required, and the need to consider alternate forms of representation and dissemination for an expanding audience from beyond the academy (Finley, 2005:682).

The 1980s and 1990s were therefore critical in shaping and directing the course of evolving arts-related research. Researchers followed their creative process as their research method, letting research and creativity unfold (Savin-Baden & Major, 2013:289). As interest in arts-related methodologies has grown the field has become much broader and complex, and whereas arts-related and collaborative research methods have originally been viewed at the margins, approaches are moving more into the mainstream as evidenced in the literature (for example, Finley, 2005; Irwin & Cosson, 2004; Hesse-Biber & Leavy, 2006; Barrett & Bolt, 2007; Knowles & Cole, 2008; Liamputtong & Rumbold, 2008; etc.). The following section maps some of the key history and critical turns in the context of research reform through which arts-related research has developed. An overview of this history and our suggested critical turns are presented in Table 2.1.

*Critical Turn One: The Narrative Turn*

The 'Narrative Turn' in the fields of education and social science largely developed out of the rise of literary theory (Polkinghorne, 1988) and from the fields of ethnography (Geertz, 1988), and can be traced to the work of other scholars such as Dewey and Bruner (for additional perspectives in social science studies, see Savin-Baden & Major, 2013: 227; Czarniawska, 2004). In a special edition of *Qualitative Inquiry,* Tierney (1999:309) suggested that there has been a 'representational straightjacket that social scientists have been in for most of this century'. The shift towards the narrative gave intellectual prominence to the construction of stories, and expressive forms of language, and offered researchers approaches that could more adequately convey and present the complexity of human life, providing a rich source of insight (Geertz, 1988; MacIntyre, 1990). Whilst post-positivist modes of knowing focused more upon categorizations and comparisons about an event, in the narrative mode, issues of context were importantly revealed, or exhibited, along with human action (Polkinghorne, 1987). Thus narrative knowledge was viewed as a means of examining the complexity of human lives rather than adopting research approaches that sought to reach firm conclusions. Within narrative research *openings* were preferred (Ingold, 2007), with the assumption that the power of the narrative plot would be opened up as a means of negotiating meaning through 'narrative interpretations' (Bruner, 1990:67). Further, researcher self-presentation using reflexive autobiographical approaches and first person narratives gained traction within the research community and was embraced increasingly by academics across disciplines ranging from history to psychology as well as in the legal, medical and therapeutic professions (Ellis, 1995; Richardson, 1997; Ellis & Bochner, 2000; Riessman, 2001).

The narrative turn in arts-related research within education is largely linked to Eisner, who, in the late 1980s and through the 1990s, with his graduate students at Stanford University and support from the American Educational Research Association (AERA), began advocating the importance of artistic forms of

Table 2.1. Critical turns and key features

| Critical turn | Period/ theoretical paradigm | Perspective | Researcher role | Characteristics | Key lit / authors |
|---|---|---|---|---|---|
| 1. The narrative turn | Post-modern (An explicit challenge to logical positivism)<br><br>Includes constructivist thinking | A device for making sense of social action through expressive forms of language and the aesthetic story | The use of aesthetic portrayal through linguistic devices; use of narrative plot and storytelling to represent and communicate social life | Use of expressive language | Polkinghorne<br>Bruner<br>Eisner<br>Barone |
| 2. Non-linguistic Forms and Blurred Genres | Post-structural Pragmatism (Multifaceted interpretation, de-centering of discipline, Relationships between beliefs, thinking, action, interrelated positions) | The crossing over of academic disciplines or domains in order that knowledgies can intersect and integrate | The use of wider aesthetic portrayal beyond the linguistic along with discipline-based theoretical foundations and expertise.<br><br>A skill base informed by emotionality, intellect, aesthetics and identity | Alternative and innovative ways of capturing, documenting, representing, and reflecting upon experience<br>For example, story, poetry, sculpture, Ethnodrama | McNiff<br>Behar<br>Weber<br>Irwin et al<br>Springgay<br>Saldana |
| 3. Arts-related research as evolving inquiry | Constructionist (Deconstruction, dialogue, re-negotiation and reconstruction) | Thus the need for arts-related research to remain undefined | Craftsmanship, artistry, and research expertise based on use of rigorous qualitative research methodologies and more fluid and open ended research practices | Disciplined and imaginative arts practices which conform to, or reject the positioning of methodological process | Sullivan<br>Finley<br>Irwin et al |
| 4. Emergence, acceptance, disruption | Critical / emancipatory (Transformative Feminism and racial equality) | A recognition for radical, revolutionary, futuristic, participative, action-orientated research practice that is ethical, political, and culturally responsive | Experiences of passion, communion, and social responsibility<br>Sensory and kinesthetic knowledge | Culture and technology provide additional means to consider forms of representation | Finley<br>Harrison |

knowing grounded in the discipline of *Art Criticism* and *connoisseurship;* a means of developing arts-based research methodology for conducting inquiry in educational research (Sullivan, 2006; Cahnmann-Taylor, 2008). Eisner explored how the practice of connoisseurship, or art appreciation, could be used to develop a research approach guided by aesthetic features and he encouraged artist-researchers to focus upon existing fields of arts, including the literary fields of poetry and prose (Eisner 1991; 1998). For example, in Art Criticism the qualities, meanings, and significance of a situation could be made visible through the lens of the artist-researcher, through the dimensions of description, interpretation, evaluation and theory generation (Eisner, 1991, 1992, 1998). Eisner's work and ideas about the future of art and research gained interest and societies such as the Arts Based Research Institute and Arts Based Educational Research (ABER) grew. Indeed ABER has continued to gain profile and membership internationally as a special interest group within the American Educational Research Association, providing a community for those who view education through artistic lenses, who use a variety of arts-based methodologies, and who communicate understandings through diverse genres (with additional subgroups).

Around the mid 1990's, Barone, Eisner's student, recognized the importance of expressive forms of language and the aesthetic story, and built on Art Criticism to develop *Narrative Construction* (Barone, 1995, 2001, 2008; Barone & Eisner, 1997) and *Narrative Story-Telling*, a new arts-based research methodology. Narrative Construction involved the researcher taking the stance as a connoisseur, who undertook profound examination of the issues under investigation, revealing details that the casual observer may overlook. 'Touching Eternity' (Barone, 2001) depicts Barone's research journey from Educational Criticism to Narrative Story-telling.

Whilst Eisner's work was controversial within the educational community, it secured a place for the arts in academic research, but there was opposition to this distinctive approach to inquiry (Barone & Eisner, 2006). However, others followed with ideas of ways to combine aesthetic expression with systematic research (for example, Lawrence-Lightfoot, 1983; Aldridge 1989, 1990). Along with ABER, other groups of scholars coalesced such as the Ontario Institute for Studies in Education, at University of Toronto 1998, who explored, articulated and sought to bring together art and social science research. In 2000 the Centre for Arts Informed Research (CAIR) was established, a centre committed to promoting innovative research using the arts in scholarly work for the purpose of advancing knowledge. This group continues to provide a context for emerging and established researchers to explore methodological issues associated with arts-informed research and offers opportunities for public access to alternative forms of research (Snowbel, 2008).

Whilst the 1980s and 1990s were critical direction of arts-related research as we know it today, this period saw linguistic forms as the main focus of research inquiry, and the majority of contributions concentrated on the use of analysis of literary art forms, with less attention being given to the use of music and the visual arts (Cahnmann-Taylor, 2008:6). Arguably the linguistic turn of postmodernism disrupted the assumption that the relationship between the artwork and the audience was a straightforward act of encoding and decoding visual forms (Sullivan, 2006). Rather, through deconstructions of identities, a powerful means of engaging people's feelings facilitated the opening up of new lines of inquiry.

Despite a growing adoption of arts-based methods by qualitative researchers, tensions existed in the field towards embracing the arts. There were few, if any, explicit references to the arts in research before 1980 (Cahnmann-Taylor 2008:5). Yet, education researchers and others within the social sciences were undeterred and ignored 'the science-over-art hierarchy' (Barone, 2012:x). Instead, increasing numbers of researchers and scholars turned to alternative forms of data representation such as symbolic and interpretative forms, as in narrative and visual data, and to approaches firmly rooted in the arts and humanities (Suppes et al., 1998:34). Such forms included painting, photography, collage, music, sculpture, film and dance which resulted in a critical (post-modern) turn in the field and new trends for social science research which required a skill base informed by emotionality, intellect, aesthetics and identity (Barone & Eisner, 1997).

## Critical Turn Two: Non-linguistic Forms and Blurred Genres

This second turn embraced experimentation of non-linguistic forms of the arts as alternative ways of representing research data. Researchers had become disenchanted with the idea of truth, objectivity and absolute knowledge and both artist researchers and social science researchers sought meanings that were partial, incomplete, even contradictory and originating from multiple perspectives (Barone, 2001).

During this period those involved in arts-related research undertook a critical philosophical move, which essentially was an epistemological turn which represented a shift in the way knowledge was conceptualized. Thus, arts-related research offered opportunities for researchers to present alternative and innovative ways of capturing, documenting, representing, and reflecting upon experience. This shift began to overthrow the dominance of technical rationality with the assumption that precise measurement was the only way to know. Whilst not seeking to discard scientific research, arts-related research recognized there was no monopoly on ways to inquire (Eisner, 2002). Arts-related research recognized that what counted as knowledge depended on perspective, time, interest and forms of representation. As a result, during the 1990s and into the 2000s, arts-related researchers continued to pioneer the use of the arts, taking risks, working with genres of poetry, painting and drama. Qualitative researchers in the social sciences became more confident that arts-related methods were relevant and this stance enabled researchers to engage with, and convey knowledge through multi-sensory means and explore new dimensions of arts-based methods.

Art-based research also emerged from arts therapy in the fields of psychiatry and psychology. Creative art therapist McNiff (1992; 2003; 2007) investigated artistic

19

processes with the field of psychology using art as the primary mode of inquiry. McNiff (2007) was interested in intertwining the heuristic, introspective qualities of artistic expression with professional practice to revive partnerships between art and science. For McNiff (2009), artistic and scientific knowing were two complementary approaches for generating creative intelligence, fostering more open and diverse ways of perceiving problems and 'dislodging' ingrained perspectives. McNiff recognized that when the systematic process of scientific inquiry was used with an art enhancing process of discovery, an empirical approach was enabled which was able to be 'responsive to the unexpected'. Yet he remained critical of researchers adopting rigid methods of inquiry, rather, he argued insights should emerge from 'sustained reflections on phenomena' (McNiff, 2007:47).

For social scientists the idea of researching human experience through the arts made sense for using visual, performative methods as a way of enhancing and disseminating social science research (Jones, 2012). The benefits of cross-disciplinary communication between social science and the arts prompted social scientists to look beyond their own philosophical groundings toward aesthetic means of representation (Jones, 2006) and a new wave of social science researchers emerged. Story, poetry, sculpture, and ethnodrama were used and along with experimental science, yet non-linguistic forms of arts-related research presented a further challenge to research traditionalists. The ability to use poetry, music, the visual arts required skills, knowledge of techniques, and a respect about the way in which the various art form was used. Thus the arts-related researcher needed to be able to convey the critical relationships between the research question, research participants, data, and use of art form to reveal what was intended (Eisner, 2008:7).

In addition to researchers using the arts and crossing disciplinary borders, in the 2000s, hybrid forms such as 'blurred genres', ScolARTistrry and A/R/Tography were embraced by social science researchers through the integration of arts-based methods and methodologies (Cahnmann-Taylor, 2008; Lea, Belliveau, Wager & Beck 2011). Blurred genres is defined here as the ways in which scholars combine discipline-based theoretical and empirical knowledge, expertise and use of the art form in ways that enliven their practices and perspectives. More than moving disputed borders and marking out a broader landscape, blurred genres prompted ways to 'think about the way we think' (Geertz, 1988). Blurred genres therefore opened up opportunities for fluid, plural, and 'untidy' diversely constructed works, which brought with them novelty, tropes and imageries of explanation (Geertz, 1988).

A/R/Tography (Irwin, 2004; Irwin & de Cosson, 2004) emerged as an arts and education practice based research methodology, identifying the artist, researcher and teacher in a collective relationship of 'knowing, doing and making' (Irwin, 2004). The artist-researcher/teacher perspective prompted a 'methodology of situations' through the combined act of creating/inquiring/ learning; a means of 'moving in and out, and around 'the work' as well as making connections in a personal way' (Irwin, Beer, Springgay et al, 2006). The authors refer to this process as the 'rhizomatic relations of a/r/togrpahy,' (Irwin et al, 2006:70), which we suggest promotes transdisciplinary knowledge as the artist/researcher/teacher explores thinking which transcends any one particular (disciplinary) realm. Further, Irwin and Springgay (2008) suggest rhizomes:

> activate the in-between; the interstitial spaces of art making, researching and teaching' through a process which 'becomes inter-textually and multiply located in the context of discursive operations. (p. 106)

Thus a central focus of A/R/Tography involves practitioners managing the tensions between living inquiry, artistic knowing and praxis in (re)questioning their understandings (Springgay et al., 2005). Further, distinct 'renderings' are used as conceptual organizers to interpret qualities observed within the creative, artistic process, focusing attention on:

1. Contiguity: the spaces in-between art, education, and research, in between 'art' and 'graphy', and in-between art and a/r/t
2. Living Inquiry: the complexity and contradictions of relations between people, things, and understandings of life experiences
3. Openings: dialogue and discourse
4. Metaphor and Metonymy: new connections and intertwined relationships
5. Reverberations: shifts in new meaning, new awareness, and new discoveries
6. Excess: what lies outside the acceptable

(Irwin & Springgay, 2008, xxvii-xxxi)

Not to be confused with methods, renderings refer to coming closer to an idea through the process of art-making (Lea et al., 2011). For example, Graham and Goetz Zwirn (2010) examined the art practice of art teachers in K-12 education to question how being an active artist contributed to, or detracted from their work as teachers. Using A/R/Tography as a framework in examining art making, researching and teaching, the inquiry process revealed that artistic practice significantly influenced the complex interactions between the subject, teacher and student, cultivating conversations, creating a safe space for engaging with students in unstructured creativity and thus establishing a context for artistic, playful exploration. Along with teacher narratives, the classroom spaces where also viewed as sites of inquiry in which the relationship between the teacher's 'studio work' and students' ability to carve out their own working space and interests could be explored.

In other examples, ScholARTistry, Nielsen (2005), has emerged as a hybrid practice of literary, visual and the performing arts with social science research methods to explore the human condition. The aim of ScholARTistry was to draw from both the social sciences and the arts to make new sense of data, during and beyond the research process, as well as reaching out to larger audiences and enabling what Barone referred to as 'truly dialogical conversations about educational possibilities' (2008:44). ScholARTristy also seeks to 'prod and pull at audiences' (Faltis 2013:59), engendering new connections and touching new emotions as evidenced in the following example:

> ### *Example*
>
> Faltis (2013) adopted ScholArtistry to bring attention to the removal of borders, not only in a physical sense, but also from the many borders that exist which prevent Mexican and other Latino immigrants from gaining full access to life, liberty and citizenship, including the right to meaningful education in America. Through the use of historical accounts tracing Mexican – US connections outlining political tensions, with vivid oil paintings representing the separation of peoples and nations, Faltis prompts the viewer and reader to re-examine education without borders from a hybrid lens of art and scholarship. Whilst depicting immigrant suffering, the paintings and text are offered as a means of questioning the wisdom of Borders and engendering new connections where people can live and learn together.

Behar (2007) provides a similar style of ScholARTistry in her work using blurred genres with ethnography, drawing on poetry and filmmaking to explore ways of how knowledge (including moral and political decision making) is realized about oneself and others. Behar (2008) argued that intellectual insights occur best when research and life worlds collide, opening up new forms of dialogue which enable communication across borders, nationality, class and faith. Behar's work seeks to validate the role of imagination in intellectual inquiry by drawing on established theories from art, politics, feminist theory and religious studies along with artful creativity. In this way the intellectual voice is extended through use of the creative, personal, observational and textual voice.

Saldaña's (2005) work as a qualitative researcher with experience of both traditional re-presentation of data as well as ethno dramatic work demonstrates how methodological approaches can meet and blend. Saldaña's use of theatre performance offers a means of representing research participants' experiences along with the researcher's interpretations of the inquiry process. This work not only prompts the viewer to examine the handling of a research question in a radically different way, engaging both scholarly communities as well as the wider public, but also in attending to the play, the viewer is able to participate vicariously in the experiences of others as prior knowledge is infused with new possibilities.

Whilst the 1980s and 1990s were critical in shaping and directing the course of evolving arts-related research, the period stretching into this last decade is arguably one in which researchers have experimented and taken greater risks with the creative process, along with personal and disciplinary perspectives, letting research and creativity unfold. Yet, arts-related research methodologies were (and remain) in conflict, with much debate about their acceptance, (Cahnmann-Taylor & Siegesmund, 2008:7). Arguably this tension presents challenges about boundary crossing, prompting researchers to ask critical questions about the use of art as an accepted mode of inquiry and to debate in what contexts art is equal to, if even more profoundly appropriate than science, as a way of understanding (Finley, 2005).

*Critical Turn Three: Arts-related Research as Evolving Inquiry*

The third critical turn comprises two major shifts characterized by opposing positions. First, the need to develop methods and to build theories and models to enhance research practice that is theoretically and methodologically robust; Second, the desire for arts-related research to remain undefined, non-paradigmatic and discipline-less (Sullivan, 2006). Those researchers advocating the latter perspective reject structured forms of methodology which may limit that which can be known. Rather, they see arts-related research as inquiry that unfolds, is fluid, and leads to new, diverse forms of knowledge production, through novel artistic strategies as the researcher and the researched are open to be changed by the creative, critical and reflexive process. From a different perspective Finley (2005), a critical arts-based researcher, has aligned arts-related research with investigate approaches that emphasize unfolding inquiry as seen in qualitative research, advocating its use as a means of social investigation and as a tool for political activism (Greenwood, 2012).

Whilst artist researchers use strategies and methods borrowed from the qualitative tradition through reflective practice, action research, grounded theory and participant observation, it is evident that researchers have also sought to refine research strategies drawn from long-stranding working methods and practices from the creative disciplines. Gray (1996) suggests these have a number of defining features centered around:

- The primacy of the creative experience
- The desire to build epistemologies of practice
- The need to improve both the practice and theoretical understandings of creative practice, and
- The opportunity to embrace the complex and emergent conditions under which practice-led researchers operate

There is therefore a push for researchers interested in strengthening arts-related practices to locate artistic research within the theories and practices that surround art making rather than selecting methods offered by the social sciences (Sullivan, 2010). Haseman and Mafe (2009) similarly highlight the tension between recognizing the value of research, yet the challenge of working with an appropriate research methodology with the assumptions, regulations and expectations imposed by the 'research industry' (p.212). As Sullivan (2006:20) contends arts-related methods need to be rigorous, but at the same time inventive, so as to reveal: 'the rich imaginative intellect as it is encountered and enacted within individual, social and cultural settings'.

It is evident that creative practice and education research methodologies such as A/R/Togrpahy, continue to develop; to examine issues of process, application and potential (Irwin, 2014).Whilst expansion of inquiry is encouraged, the question of how such practices can be embraced within existing research paradigms is questioned. Denzin argues that a confidence is required within the field to follow different yet complementary pathways to create knowledge production.

> Further, he suggests that arts-based researchers should be open to vernacular, folk, and popular culture forms; to include outsider art; and to allow variance from conventional art practice in the art world as much as encourage departure from prevailing conventions of social science research (summarized from Denzin, 2000: 258)

Clearly, there is a range of perspectives about the ways in which arts-related research should evolve, not least in terms of the aesthetic dimension such research brings forth, which is complex, dynamic, culturally situated, multi-faceted, emergent, ambiguous, visceral, emotional, intuitive and essentially nonverbal (Greenwood, 2012:17). However, it would appear a clear message is emerging about research practice with the arts, which we suggest centers on the desire to retain the uncertainty and playfulness of the creative process, whilst ensuring theoretical and philosophical perspectives draw on the substantial history and frameworks of meaning underpinning creative arts practice.

*Critical Turn Four: Emergence, Acceptance, Disruption*

The fourth critical turn locates the field in contemporary practice and is where this text, through the following chapters, picks up the 'trail'; an example of this is provided by Ewing, below:

---

***Author Reflection***
***Robyn Ewing***, Professor of Teacher Education and the Arts, Faculty of Education and Social Work, University of Sydney.

Arts-informed research methodologies are innovative qualitative approaches to research that in my experience are being used increasingly in Australian education and social work research projects. Termed 'third space methodologies' (O'Toole & Beckett, 2010), they provoke a disruption of conventional and taken-for-granted ways of thinking about knowledge and research, and enable the exploration of research questions, dilemmas, issues or experiences that touch on the liminal nature and complexities of our professions.

Imaginative literary, visual and performing processes and artistry can help 'perceive patterns in new ways, find sensuous openings into new understandings, fresh concepts, wild possibilities...subvert the ordinary and see the extraordinary' (Neilsen, 1998, p. 274). Barone (2001) drew attention to the

---

*Continued*

value of arts-informed research in exploring educational issues. Writing about the teacher who is the subject of his book Touching Eternity he discusses the:

> enormously complex, wide ranging, highly ambiguous, profoundly personal, unquestionably social, intrinsically political and inevitably subjective nature of the outcomes of teaching and learning. Nevertheless the process of searching for these answers may offer the pleasantly unexpected: the appearance of additional questions quite numerous and splendid. (pp. 1–2)

As Hughes and I (2008) argued, these methodologies seem most appropriate when exploring 'liminal' kinds of research questions, places where disparate cultures, ideologies and frameworks may meet' (Conroy, 2004: 54). It is my belief that arts-informed approaches are more appropriate for investigating those research questions or issues that involve the practices and lived experiences of individuals allowing the complexities and boundaries of these practices to be explored. Several recent examples of research studies using arts-informed research are briefly described below.

Teaching style is very much related to the identity of the individual, yet this personal-professional identity is difficult to articulate. Victoria Campbell used oral storying with early career primary teachers to explore the development of their professional and personal identities, as well as their emerging pedagogies. The participants created a dramatic oral performance using the framework of The Seal Wife to investigate their early teaching experiences. Campbell demonstrated that finding one's own authentic voice through a creative storying activity was empowering for early career teachers, enabling them to establish a more resilient professional identity. This is important, given the high attrition rate of teachers in their first three to five years of teaching.

– Linda Hodson chose to investigate the practices of two teacher educators recognized as outstanding, in order to develop an understanding of the role of affect and emotion in quality tertiary teaching. She explored the insights and experiences that informed their ways of engaging with preservice teachers and reciprocally, how these preservice teachers experienced these pedagogies. She used narrative, poetry, metaphor and other literary devices to represent her findings.
– Kirsty McGeoch used digital storytelling in her teaching of English courses to enable newly arrived students. Her research demonstrates how the students' creation of their own digital stories enabled them to develop rich cultural understandings and tolerance of each other while learning academic English.
– Nikki Bunker used portraiture and patchwork to explore how well primary teachers in one school supported the social and emotional wellbeing of children in their care whilst grappling with a neoliberal emphasis on narrow academic achievement. She created a patchwork quilt to represent how the academic discourse had been separated from that of social and emotional wellbeing.

## CONCLUSION

Whilst the traditions of the arts as teaching and investigative tools stretch back throughout history, the use of the creative arts as formal methodological approaches to academic research is relatively new. Debate continues about ways of theorizing and locating arts-related research approaches. This chapter has attempted to trace the origins of arts-related research in terms of its historical and disciplinary development. It has explored the processes and practices that have informed its development and examined such shifts in practices through considerations of a critical turns which provide opportunity to appreciate how trends and differences have occurred, and are occurring within the field.

# UNDERTAKING ARTS-RELATED RESEARCH

## INTRODUCTION

In this chapter the reasons for deciding to use arts-related research will be considered. This includes formulating a purpose for the research in terms of considering the research question, together with an appropriate type of arts-related inquiry. The importance of researcher positioning and collaboration with other research team members will also be discussed, along with pragmatic constraints such as time, space and the organizational issues involved, not least in locating and recruiting research participants and working with stakeholder groups. Finally, consideration of factors affecting the relationship between the researcher, research participants and creative productivity will be discussed.

## UNDERTAKING ARTS-RELATED RESEARCH

It is important to understand why arts-related research should be used as a methodology of choice in the first instance. Having a love of the arts or having expertise in a particular art form are not reason enough, nor should this approach be used because it appears to be straightforward to implement. Decisions about using arts-related research should focus on how arts-related research reveals the value of an *aesthetic dimension*, and how this may enhance both the research process and representational phases, in ways that other research approaches do not.

In developing the inquiry and research focus, initial questions need to be asked about why the study is required and what particular practice concerns in the field are worthy of exploration, who this will interest, and how might it reach and be received by new and diverse audiences beyond the academic. The following issues should be considered in undertaking arts-related research:

- Formulating a research question
- The artist and researcher
- Working with participants and stakeholders

### Formulating a Research Question

Researchers with experience in qualitative inquiry questioning why they might wish to use arts-related research should consider what this approach will offer, which goes beyond conventional social science research with its aim to understand a phenomenon. Arts-related research also offers opportunities to explore an issue or question, yet rather than seeking to explain, or search for answers, it may more importantly offer potential to disrupt, open up, provoke, or present the phenomenon in a 'dislocated form' (Smith & Dean, 2009). The focus is on looking afresh at a phenomenon; to 'unflatten' it (Sousanis, 2013); to examine and portray the iterative relationships between the issue, the context, the researcher and the participants, through creative multi-dimensional work. Further, arts-related research offers a variable and powerful means of examining political, social and moral concerns and conveying emotional complexities through expressive means of (re)presentation, which are able to be shared with wide audiences (Seeley & Reason, 2008).

Along with enlivening research practice for social science researchers, arts-related research also offers approaches for artists to examine their own practice, which has the potential to open new avenues of knowledge, not least in redefining what contribution to knowledge an 'artwork' makes. As argued by Hecq and Banagan (2009), just because an artwork has been produced does not mean it is ground-breaking in terms of knowledge production. In formulating a purpose therefore, it is important to consider what forms of aesthetic knowing will be considered of benefit for methodological, procedural and even political change.

In Table 3.1 below, we provide a typology of arts-related research practice as outlined in Chapter 1, and provide examples of how researchers might locate their approach for undertaking arts-related research relative to the type of inquiry and its key characteristics. Suggestions for the focus of research questions is linked to each type of inquiry, including how the inquiry can contribute to, and inform, ways of knowing.

As Table 3.1 outlines, the use of a typology of arts-related research can provide a means of considering how an arts-related research project will be undertaken and shaped in line with a researcher's philosophical and theoretical orientation, (as discussed previously in Chapter 1) for example, a constructivist or constructionist perspective. Whilst the arts-related researcher may feel concern about *closing down* what has potential to *unfold* during the inquiry process, we suggest that by locating the purpose of the study and its design within a particular approach, the researcher is able to convey the contribution to knowledge that arts-related research can make and thus deepen the impact of the research (Daykin, 2008; Piercy et al., 2005). Further, being transparent about a starting position does not preclude any shifts in stance which may occur. Such shifts can then be accounted for in the dissemination and presentation of the inquiry.

Another way to formulate an arts-related research question would be to identify the issue or concern in a particular context, to consider the types and characteristics of arts-related research methodologies listed in Tables 3.2 to 3.7, and to work through the following factors to help locate the inquiry, as exemplified overleaf:

*Table 3.1. Formulating a research question*

| Type | Key characteristics | Suggested focus for research questions | Contribution to knowledge |
|---|---|---|---|
| **Arts-inquiring pedagogy** | Use of the artistic process to teach inquiry and enable learning through exploration | How can the artistic process be used to improve teaching? | Advancing knowledge about learning, teaching and practice. New knowledge that has pedagogical and practical significance |
| **Arts-based inquiry** | The ways in which the artistic process is used by artists, researchers and participants to understand the art itself or to understand a phenomenon | How can different art forms be used in different ways, for example to sustain and improve or express states of mind, confidence and self-esteem? Or, What can the artist learn about the technical aspects of the artistic process, and issues of portrayal through inquiry? | Making and creating through art forms as a means of understanding personal growth and development of practice. |
| **Arts-informed inquiry** | The use of art to represent the findings of a study to enhance understanding and reach multiple audiences. The use of art to represent a response to the findings of an issue or situation studied | How can the use of an art form represent a narrative? Or, How can the analysis and interpretation of interview or focus group data be (re)presented in ways to promote visual-verbal inquiry? | New forms of representation and generation of new forms of response |
| **Arts-informing inquiry** | Art is used in order to evoke a response from an audience (in the broadest sense) made to a situation or issue; the response may or may not be captured. | How can 'performance' be used to explore perspectives about an issue or phenomena? | New knowledge about emotional and embodied responses to art |
| **Arts-engaging inquiry** | The use of art to engage communities and marginalized groups | How can issues and concerns, pertinent to a particular group or community, be voiced or portrayed to prompt action? | Knowledge about how art can be used to mobilise, enable and support community action |
| **Arts-related evaluation** | The use of the artistic process to undertake, represent and disseminate evaluation research. | How can art be used to evaluate a programme or event? | Knowledge of challenges and success through the artistic process |

*Table 3.2. Question formulation for arts-inquiring pedagogy*

| | |
|---|---|
| **Subject** | Maths Education |
| **Issue** | Student's ability to persist with working out complex maths problems |
| **Focus** | How can the artistic process be used as a form of pedagogy? |
| **Type** | Arts-inquiring pedagogy |
| **Contribution to knowledge** | Advancing knowledge about learning, teaching and practice. New knowledge that has pedagogical and practical significance. |
| **Question** | How can the artistic process aid problem-solving in students studying maths in higher education? |

*Table 3.3. Example question formulation for arts-based inquiry*

| | |
|---|---|
| **Subject** | Post-graduate music programme |
| **Issue** | Musical composition |
| **Focus** | Exploring an area of technical skill development through the artistic process |
| **Type** | Arts-based inquiry |
| **Contribution to knowledge** | Making and creating through art forms as a means of understanding personal growth and development of practice |
| **Question** | What semiotic aspects of musical meaning can be identified to develop music practice? |

*Table 3.4. Example question formulation for arts-informed inquiry*

| | |
|---|---|
| **Subject** | Allied health professional programme |
| **Issue** | Career trajectory and issues of professional identity development |
| **Focus** | To explore the ways an art form could be used as a means of support analysis, interpretation and representation of research data |
| **Type** | Arts-informed inquiry |
| **Contribution to knowledge** | New forms of representation and generation of new forms of response |
| **Question** | How can digital storytelling represent undergraduates' ideas of their career trajectory? |

*Table 3.5. Example question formulation for arts-informing inquiry*

| | |
|---|---|
| **Subject** | Voice and presence of older adults |
| **Issue** | Educate and broaden understanding about the needs and wishes of older people including perspectives on ageing |
| **Focus** | To elicit heightened awareness of ageing for those viewing the 'performance' and how such work may simulate life experience or theatrically 'fictionalise' it |
| **Type** | Arts-informing inquiry |
| **Contribution to knowledge** | New knowledge about emotional, and embodied responses to art |
| **Question** | How can dance be used as a means of understanding older people's perspectives on ageing? |

*Table 3.6. Example question formulation for arts-engaging inquiry*

| | |
|---|---|
| **Subject** | Youth education programme |
| **Issue** | To explore reasons for disengagement and rising attrition rates with young people attending the programme |
| **Focus** | To explore the concerns or issues pertinent to a group or community |
| **Type** | Arts-engaging inquiry |
| **Contribution to knowledge** | Knowledge about how art can be used to mobilize, enable and support community action |
| **Question** | How can the use of the Spoken Word and poetry be used within a community youth programme to examine the needs of its young people? |

*Table 3.7. Example question formulation for arts-related evaluation*

| | |
|---|---|
| **Subject** | Evaluation of a peer to peer mentoring programme |
| **Issue** | The use of aesthetic techniques to present the breadth of participant data |
| **Focus** | How can evaluators express their creativity as a central means of portraying the evaluation of a phenomenon or issue? |
| **Type** | Arts-related evaluation |
| **Contribution to knowledge** | Knowledge of challenges and successes through the artistic process |
| **Question** | How can the use of an arts installation be used to evaluate a peer to peer mentoring programme? |

*The Artist and Researcher*

It is the arts-related researcher's role to be as transparent as possible about the process and reasons for conducting an inquiry. Being aware of one's own researcher stance, relative to the purpose of the inquiry is crucial, especially if the focus of concern is related to the researcher's own professional background. Thus self-awareness and self-disclosure are important responsibilities for the artist and researcher to address. Thus periods of reflexivity should be undertaken to iteratively reflect upon how the research process and researcher's stance will impact upon the 'making' and reporting of the study findings. This is exemplified by Cutcher:

---

**Author Reflection**
**Alexandra Cutcher**, School of Education, Southern Cross University, Australia.

Arts-based research is not for everyone. I believe it should only be employed if the sensibility of the researcher and the requirements of the research demand it. As a pragmatist, I don't believe that this is a method that fits every type of educational research by every researcher. It is simply a matter of what works best for both. For me, as an artist and a teacher and a writer, it is a good fit. It requires sensitivity, good judgement, an ironic posture that doesn't take itself too seriously, and a great deal of organisation, rigour and discipline. It is not for the fainthearted, and it is a tremendous amount of work. Yet, it is wonderfully invigorating and in itself, very satisfying. Although these things are not the purposes of research, they certainly motivate the researcher to continue with the work, and that in itself is a useful outcome.

It is very difficult to give a 'how to do arts-based research' address, seminar or workshop, because like the art that supports and represents it, arts-based research is gloriously idiosyncratic. The highly personal nature of arts-based research is one of its greatest strengths – its particularity, its depth, and its success in mining these characteristics for new ways of seeing the universal are facilitated through a distinctive discourse (Diamond and Mullen, 2000). Everybody's practice, thinking, feeling and intentions are as individual and as enigmatic as the subjective self from which they are exhumed. In my research I have always trusted in the process (McNiff, 1998), and this intuition has never failed me. I work through a combination of both systematic and rigorous enterprise, coupled with instinct. In my research, as in my art and my teaching, I believe that both approaches are required. Discipline is also absolutely necessary, since a constant and very self-aware approach is crucial to the success of this type of research. Time is an issue; harnessing creative energies, acquiring the vast amount of information that research processes yield, and sifting through these souvenirs to find the pearls, requires a lot of time, space and organisation.

---

*Continued*

All research is interpretive, but arts-based inquiries are very self-conscious. I am constantly aware of the method, how I should, could and will use it, what criticisms it can engender and how to present the information. A healthy scepticism and an ironic posture have also been helpful tools. My ability not to take myself seriously at times, and to welcome the criticism of others, especially non-academics, has been of enormous benefit.

It is essential for me to be very structured and organised in the construction of my research. I find it necessary to keep both mental and physical records of where it is going. It is vital to be multitask-oriented. On the other hand, it is also necessary to allow the work to 'breathe', and whilst I am aware that this sounds very esoteric, it is an artistic truth for me. It is like navel gazing, a highly underrated enterprise, and to be able to use this consciously I have had to make space for chance and serendipity to play a part, and create the mental space for the 'truths' to emerge. It is important to trust that the subconscious mind will deliver the goods, but only if one is disciplined about it. These seemingly contradictory devices and qualities are the charming, and somewhat unknowable, elements of arts-based research. Structure as well as chaos, discipline as well as madness, are an integral part of this method for me.

In addition to self-reflective questioning and shifts in positioning as the inquiry process unfolds, the arts-related researcher needs to reflect on their own knowledge of the field, and their intellectual and creative interests. The researcher also needs to consider what is of interest to a particular audience as well as which forms of 'credible evidence' will elicit a response. By this we mean how plausible, convincing or sincere the use of the visual, symbolic, digital, and narrative might be in addressing the issue under investigation.

The arts-related researcher undertakes many roles, such as to critique, challenge, uncover and create (Siegesmund and Cahnmann-Taylor, 2008). These roles require the researcher to live with the liminal and to manage a position of not knowing, feeling lost and recognizing that this research in invariably ambiguous, multidimensional and involves finding flow. The concept of finding flow is based on the work of Csikszentmihalyi (1996; 2002). Flow is that state of engagement in a skilful and challenging task, where time seems to fly by. The examples he has cited in particular are driving and mountaineering. In mountaineering and specifically in rock climbing there is sense that the moves flow, with ease, grace and rhythm. Csikszentmihalyi defines flow as:

> … being completely involved in an activity for its own sake. The ego falls away. Time flies. Every action, movement, and thought follows inevitably from the previous one, like playing jazz. Your whole being is involved, and you're using your skills to the utmost. (Csikszentmihalyi, 1996:1)

33

There is a sense of 'finding flow' (Csikszentmihalyi, 1996) that is also captured by Woolf, who offers a poignant example in relation to writing:

> One day walking around Tavistock Square I made up, as I sometimes make up my books, *To the Lighthouse*; in a great, apparently involuntary rush. One thing burst into another. Blowing bubbles out of a pipe gives the feeling of the rapid crowd of ideas and scenes which blew out of my mind, so that my lips seemed syllabling of their own accord as I walked. What blew the bubbles? Why then? I have no notion. But I wrote the book very quickly... (Woolf, 1940: 92)

Whilst the experience of being in a time and space when a sense of flow emerges spontaneously may happen to few of us, there are other times when flow occurs during the artistic process and in the interpretation of data. There is a belief that just by allowing the unconscious self to write, create, paint, dance then flow will occur, so that there is a sense of 'suspension of disbelief.' Thus the arts-related researcher needs to question and to suspend their disbelief in order to prompt, widen and deepen conversations. The researcher should see themselves as a conduit for broadening dialogues and opening up the research landscape through use of a creative and questioning approach.

There has been much discussion about who can take on the role of the arts-related researcher, and what issues they need to consider, and whether those without an artistic background should be discouraged from adopting it. The roles that require consideration are:

– Artist as researcher
– Researcher without an arts background

*Artist as researcher* — We define artist as researcher as a person educated and trained within the arts, with knowledge inherent in art practice as found within the creative process (Blom, 2006; Hannan, 2006) and the creative outcome (Bolt, 2006; Crossman, 2006), and who works and practices with aesthetic forms, such as visual art, theatre, ceramics, poetry, dance, music or digital image, sound, and interactive multimedia. Those trained in the arts possess a number of characteristics that equip them for the role of artist-researcher:

– Artistic willingness to disrupt and dislodge perspectives to take up alternative lines of inquiry
– The valuing of critical perspectives, play, and sensual communication with audiences
– Artistic valuing of creativity and innovation so that new perspectives might be applied to inquiries, incorporating criteria such as celebration and wonder
– The experience of 'being within' (rather than abstracted from) the arts practice, and researching through and within that practice.

Often, but not always, the artist is the researcher and the researcher the artist, with the position of the artist and researcher depending on the type of arts-related approach adopted (as considered within the typology outlined in Chapter 1).The artist as researcher approach arguably enables an understanding to emerge through the researcher being equipped within the discipline, to talk about the work as a creator of work, of art and art practice; to assume the mantle of both artist and critic (Siegesmund and Cahnmann-Taylor, 2008). The artist as researcher offers an in-depth means of interplay; a role for imagination, reliance on metaphorical thinking and openness to the visions of human possibility (Greene, 1998).

This ability of the researcher's own interconnectedness with the subject matter; the idea of 'bricolage,' (Savin-Baden and Major, 2013) provides an important means for the arts-related researcher to highlight relationships which become apparent through knowledge of material processes, art discourse and creative praxis. This contribution of the artistic with the investigative is illustrated in the following excerpt, by an artist-researcher as participant involved in an action research-based theatre project:

> As an arts-based researcher I constantly seek ways to bring art within my research. In this project I wanted to see what might emerge if we used an intense theatre process to both develop and disseminate our research. The goal was not to create a reader's theatre script, but instead we wanted to embody the data, move beyond words to include the kinaesthetic and visceral. We wanted to workshop the script and then rehearse it so the artistic would be honoured, balancing it with the research data that represented our content. (White & Belliveau, 2011:227)

The materials, methods and theoretical ideas are thus viewed as the tools from which the research design and artistic process emerges. This 'knowledge nexus' (Bennett et al., 2010), influenced by disciplinary regimes and the artist's experience and practice of experimentation and re-imaginings, will influence cultural reproduction; or the process of reflecting on one's development (with others), and communicating new understandings through intuitive work drawing upon contextual and artistic foundations.

Yet, as arts-related research goes beyond making art (Smith, 2002; Ewing and Hughes, 2008), the artist as researcher is not the sole creator of meaning for arts-related research, as the juxtaposition of ideas and co creation is after all an intrinsic part of creativity.

*Researcher without an arts background* — Researchers from the social sciences are always looking for viable means to engage others with their research, in ways that can effectively capture and convey emotional complexities that significantly shape an investigation into the human condition (White and Belliveau, 2011). As arts-related research has increasingly borrowed approaches such as action research and participatory or co-operative inquiry, qualitative researchers well versed in such approaches are naturally reciprocally interested to adopt arts-related approaches to question, broaden and expand the scope of their own inquiry (Liamputtong and Rumbold, 2008).

Further, drawing on propositional knowledge outside the arts, researchers without an arts background bring forth other theoretical underpinnings and insights. The type of arts-related research that such researchers might engage with is more akin to arts-informed inquiry, also referred to by Ewing and Hughes (2008:516) as 'expressive construction', the focus being to communicate new understandings through creative means, yet without those creative means being considered as works of art.

Whilst those new to the field of arts-related research may be interested in how the arts can enrich and extend qualitative methodologies and epistemologies (Daykin, 2008), tensions exist and issues of quality and representation remain. As Daykin (2008: 233) highlights, the concern not to 'contaminate' and to 'protect art' from the 'social' is still present for some artists. Claims such as Carey's (2005: 9) which suggest that 'a work of art is anything anyone has considered a work of art, though it may be a work of art only for that one person', have met with criticism from those who demand that arts-informed inquiry requires the development of robust understanding of the nature of art, both within the academy and beyond. Such unease often emanates from the way practices may result in undermining both the craft of what counts as art and the professional standing of what it means to be an artist. Further, the process of conducting arts-related research requires the researcher both to incorporate their experience, feelings, reflection and willingness to respond creatively, as well as to encourage research participants to continue to develop their relationship with the art form.

Challis, an artist working in participatory community practice reflects on her stance in relation to this:

---

*Author Reflection*
*Participatory Community Arts Practice*
**Sue Challis**, Coventry University, UK

Recognising and valuing another profession's tropes, materials and practices is fundamental to the partnership which the phrase 'arts-related inquiry' implies, and is not without (well-documented) challenges. Pain (2013) points out the danger inherent in the seductive 'instant engagement' appeal of creative research collaborations for academic researchers negotiating the 'turn to community', and the lure of academic credibility it might offer practice-based artists. As an artist relatively recently engaged in research, I am interested in the ways in which these

---

*Continued*

related practices of the artist and the researcher, both concerned with curiosity and communication, differ.

Clearly, there are different skills involved, but a more profound distinction between research and creative practice may also lie in different ways of looking at and interacting with the world. Characteristically, for the artist, it is the continual incorporation of experience, thought, feelings and the material world, through sketchbooks, journals, photographs, collages, collecting and so on, as potential artworks, and a constant, open-ended re-assembling of these, that create new relationships. This is a persistent process of experimentation, false starts, re-workings and temporary abandoning; what artist Bob and Roberta Smith calls a "mode of thinking and activity concerned with action" (Smith 2004:136). Two things follow from this process: firstly, that the starting point and the boundaries of a piece of work, may be less well-defined, or even more difficult to contain, for the artist than for the researcher. Second, that the 'selection of materials' may be a more complex process than a practical choice about content and form. This attachment to making has led me to become particularly interested in a specific kind of arts-related inquiry; that is, creative research methods, which involve participants making new artworks themselves. (I do not ask people to draw, being too aware of the danger of subverting the hierarchy of text and talk only to replace it with another related to ability and confidence). Creative research methods have implications for the experience of participation in research, and for interpretation of data. Research where the participant actively creates something new (rather than responds to existing work or prompts an artist to make work) can produce new and rich meanings.

This research data, made in response to participants' own creations, or a research question, using artist-led processes and artist-quality materials, has the potential to create aesthetic value (Frogett et al, 2011). By this I mean a thematic coherence, a non-linear and satisfying whole (Barone and Eisner 2012), with potential to become an important aspect for interpretation of the meaning of the artwork and of the process of making it. This satisfaction is perhaps a less obvious source of a creative method's ability to engage research participants - alongside its association with play and by-passing of text and talk. No more felt-tip and flipchart though: "there is an intimate connection between technology and expressivity" (Barone and Eisner, 2012:5). The experience of being creative – even in a brief research encounter - can have several positive impacts on people, connected with eudaimonic wellbeing and the production of identity (Fujiwara et al, 2014; Gauntlett, 2007).

My research (Challis 2013a, b; Challis 2014) and experience in the field of participatory community arts practice, suggests that, to maximise the impact of being creative, certain things need to be in place. If the conditions are created for

*Continued*

even the slightest acquisition of skills within a symbolic domain and the intense concentration associated with 'creative flow' (Csikzentmihaly 2002), impact is intensified. Mastering new technologies or materials (however simple), fosters the 'making strange' which contributes to the disruptive quality needed for new understanding. For me, still in the process of developing an ethical framework for this kind of research, the fact that participating in the creative research activity of itself has the potential to offer participants positive impact (for example, contribute to their greater sense of agency or wellbeing), is significant.

As I continue to struggle with the interpretation of creative data, I am convinced that, as with 'high' art, meanings are made between people; they are not inherent in the work. It is the aesthetic value of the data which suggests to me that, although visual or thematic analyses (like those used in visual cultural analysis) may be useful to identify patterns and direct research questions, asking participants to interpret their own artwork is vital: and they may use this process to construct a new narrative about the research question, or about themselves.

In order to make the best use of creative methods, researchers must use them for themselves: develop a deeper understanding of materials, technologies and creative processes, have a bit of fun, and begin to become hybrid artist-researchers.

If the artistic process is viewed as the important means of creating new relationships, then as Challis suggests, an understanding of art forms, materials and the creative process may provide important insights for those researchers thinking about if and how they might implement the approach.

*Working with Participants and Stakeholders*

In addition to formulating the research question, the arts-related researcher needs to make pragmatic decisions based on a number of parallel factors that will serve to frame the inquiry at the outset, which include:

– Locating and working with participants
– Managing resources
– Research relationships
– Engaging audience perspectives

*Locating and working with participants* — A crucial and potentially time consuming initial stage of an inquiry process is concerned with recruitment and access to the study population. This often relies on working with a range of community partners or stakeholder groups who are agreeable to promote the study through their networks. An example of this is a project, in which we were involved in evaluating the impact of arts-based activities, particularly the use of theatre and performance, on the health and wellbeing of the 50+ population in Coventry:

A project team came together consisting of representatives from the theatre, the project manager (employed to promote the project and deliver the staged intervention), Age UK (a UK based charity), city council representatives and ourselves as researchers. The project was widely promoted through local media and Age UK networks including community groups, sheltered residences, churches and charitable organizations, where taster sessions were offered which led interested participants into weekly developmental workshops. An Age UK project worker accompanied the project manager in recruiting participants. Her role could be viewed as one of a 'translator'; working with the artist and supporting the interaction with potential group members. (Wimpenny and Savin-Baden, 2014)

Establishing networks with partner organizations is a worthwhile endeavor, as arts-related research is well placed to examine issues related to community learning and inquiry, social justice, community cohesion, citizenship and wellbeing. However, to accomplish meaningful networks, community partners need to be convinced that the work is of sufficient quality to engage their commitment and endorsement at the outset. Often there are no short cut solutions and time is required to build up working relationships, so that a track record can emerge of work overseen, or developed together, which then has potential to lead to further ventures and joint funding applications.

*Author Reflection*
**Katherine Wimpenny**, Coventry University, UK

Getting the most vulnerable, marginalized, isolated people to be involved in a project presents a very real challenge, especially when working with other restrictions of time and financial support. What I have learnt is that the lead-in time to a project is significant in terms of gaining access to and recruiting participants. If effective stakeholder networks are not in place to support this process, then funding and other restrictions may mean that by the time the project actually starts, the final deadline may already be uncomfortably close.

It may be that the focus of the inquiry embraces the concerns experienced by a group, community or organization (McTaggart, 1997), and be a piece of participatory action (PAR) arts-related research which aims to be democratic, equitable, and liberating for those involved. As such, ways of conceptualising research relationships with the study participants at the outset is required. This recognizes that those involved come together in a 'communitarian way' (Lincoln 2001:127), breaking down borders between knowledge producing and knowledge consuming elites. Here the role of the arts-related researcher is one of exploring the PAR method; encouraging the development of collective decision-making, making a commitment to improvements, and considering researcher roles. Negotiating issues of power amongst individuals in the light of one another's own vision of the inquiry, its aims, methods and creative actions, and making this process amenable to all, is a task not to be underestimated. People cannot be empowered by an external agency; as Duncan (2013:256) contends, this occurs only when people as co-researchers take ownership of their personal and collective development process. When arts-related research is focused on human interaction and effective aesthetic portrayal, then it has significant potential to be transformative and empowering, as Townsend (1996:182) notes:

> Empowerment is enabled when people demonstrate mutual respect, promote positive interdependence, share risk and responsibility, encourage hope and build trust in themselves and others.

Thus, choice, information, respect and feeling heard to are important factors in promoting authentic participation, whereby individual's needs are genuinely considered and respected by the researcher and project team. Yet as easy as this is to espouse, enacting such relationships in practice is not straightforward. Equally, it is important to appreciate that participants will not hold static positions. Rather, perspectives are likely to shift as the inquiry process unfolds. Nonetheless, from the outset, all participants need to feel that they have valued roles in being involved, whether these be as more or less engaged.

What is apparent is that locating the research population is unlikely to occur in a fixed, linear process; rather, access and recruitment strategies will need to be divergent and iterative around the purpose of the inquiry. The use of a steering group may also be a useful means of working with community stakeholders during the project lifetime. The steering group's role and responsibilities may include guiding and overseeing the study and its aims (Wimpenny and Savin-Baden, 2014). Regular meetings between the researcher(s) and partners can provide opportunities for discursive relationships to develop in which interim findings can be discussed, project issues deliberated on, and meaningful ways forward considered.

Questions need to be asked about what practical, theoretical and or political research utility the study will provide and to whom. The intention of the inquiry may be to influence people's perceptions towards a particular practice, group or population. It may be the inquiry is used to inform policy makers, researchers, practitioners, or the thinking of a wider community. Having an understanding of particular practice concerns, contextually situated, including any temporal dimensions articulated in professional discourse, can provide a meaningful focus and help hone ideas. Yet equally, recognizing the various stakes of different groups can potentially sensitize the arts-related researcher. Thus the researcher needs to be aware of their stance and the ethics of how the inquiry is conducted and its findings disseminated.

> Apol (2012) used her skills as a poet to explore the experiences she witnessed as a researcher working on a writing-for-healing project, in which stories collected by Tutsi survivors of the 1994 genocide in Rwanda were used to create a literature for the children of Rwanda and the wider public. Apol was able to both explore her own experiences, as well as use her poetry to include participant testimonies and create a powerful work of art. This was made accessible to a diverse range of audiences, as a form of social action.

*Managing resources* — Maximizing the quality of the study within available resources is clearly important to achieve, both in terms of the choice of art genre to be used, for example, music, poetry, dance or photography, as well as other constraints such as materials, space, financial costs and time. Further, as identified by Bolt (2007:29):

> materials are not just passive objects to be used instrumentally by the artist, but rather the materials and processes of production have their own intelligence that comes into play in interaction with the artist's creative intelligence.

This 'material productively' requires substantial space and 'breathing time' (Cutcher, 2014) in order to achieve an effective aesthetic utility (Bolt 2007; Barone and Eisner, 2012). In addition, as well as the importance of the relationship forming between the researcher and the art form, the collaboration between the researcher and other team members is also a core element of the work.

Careful inclusion of representatives relevant to the research question and the purpose of the inquiry is required. This may include working with colleagues across education, policy, and user representatives as well as any third sector partners. Ideally individuals with knowledge of the substantive area will be involved, alongside a researcher with methodological and artistic expertise, who is able to convey meanings otherwise unavailable to those without a creative background. For example, Del Mar, a legal scholar keen to reenergise the typical text-dominated student learning of legal theory, worked closely with a visual artist and an actress. This blend of team expertise enabled Del Mar (2014) to generate new insights about legal reasoning, whilst the artists created new kinds of processes with new kinds of applications, enabling a genuine sharing of ideas.

*Research relationships* — At a preliminary level, the importance of the arts-related researcher explaining the purpose of the study in an accessible way is required. At a less tangible level is a consideration of material relationships; referring to participant engagement with the particular art form or genre being used. What is important in this relationship is a respect for the participants' autonomy and capacity to want to create. The researcher needs to appreciate the 'situation' of the other and how engagement with creative practices may have implications in terms of leaving people feeling vulnerable. This extends to both the creative process itself, and the potential of doing the unfamiliar. Reaching for new ways of expression or distilling an experience into an image or creative form may be especially powerful and disruptive for participants (Sinding et al., 2008:460).

Decisions here include how the researcher can 'manage' participants' responses which may be more embodied, visceral, or symbolic in their exchange. Sinding et al., (2008:461) suggest that arts-informed processes themselves offer unique ways to respond to distress when it emerges. The very act of singing, performing or creating can help with the intensity of feeling and enable a response to be 'contained' within the creative act itself. The researcher must be aware of their role boundaries and areas of expertise, which should be clearly delineated. For example, in her research with residents of domestic abuse refuges, Challis (2014) works with a member of refuge staff, who is there to offer follow-up attention. The voice of the arts-related researcher should not dominate or overpower the voices of the researched. This means the researcher foregoing a tone of certainty, which otherwise can prevent other possibilities and alternatives to meaning making from occurring (Barone and Eisner, 2012:135). Yet issues of vulnerability are worth considering in terms of how sharing of oneself in a creative process may link to how participants (and audiences) view the person and how this may impact on one's future. Furthermore, are individuals agreeable to losing their anonymity through identifying their work and ideas?

It is therefore important to consider to whom the work belongs, how the study findings will be disseminated, and over what time frame. The use of creative works for public presentation, exhibition and academic journals needs to be discussed openly with research participants at both the start and during the inquiry process, as forms of expression are explored and created. In summary, it is important that arts-related research is considered in ways that respect participant engagement, offer informed choice and as Gilman (1988) suggests, lend boundaries to what is often difficult to witness and convey.

*Engaging audience perspectives* — As is the intention of arts-related research, uncertainty, confrontation and risk-taking are used with a desire to provoke and present 'new' ways of thinking about particular phenomena, to engage an audience. Whilst it is challenging to anticipate how an audience might respond, the representations offered may affect those witnessing them, especially people or groups close to the subject matter, for example by undermining people's previous perspectives. Sinding et al., (2008:462) note that it is not the role of the researcher and the research participants to 'stand between the audience and the representation' as the audience are there to 'craft their own meaning'; yet equally representations have potential to do harm. Possible strategies might relate to informing audiences about the subject matter upfront in promoting the work, so as to provide informed consent to those choosing to view it.

## CONCLUSION

This chapter has considered the many overlapping and often complex decisions required when deciding to use arts-related research and starting a project. Question areas related to different *types* of arts-related inquiry have been discussed. Whilst not an exhaustive list, we have considered the work's audience, how research participants will be located and recruited, and how networks of support may be accessed through working with stakeholder groups. Further, issues about the relationship between the researcher, participant and creative productivity have been discussed, including the challenge of balancing participant choice, issues of competence in the selected art form, and maintaining respect and avoiding exploitation and vulnerability.

# WHAT ARE ARTS-RELATED METHODS?

## INTRODUCTION

This chapter will explore what counts as methods in arts-related research. It begins by examining the importance of locating methods within a paradigm and methodology, suggesting that this ensures trustworthiness and rigour in data collection. It suggests that researchers need to have a clear philosophical and researcher stance, but that such a stance is liquid and flexible to a degree. The chapter provides examples of relevant data collection techniques and suggests that arts-related methods are now used in a wide variety of ways. Examples of its use include performance, poetry, dance, drama, music and writing. These approaches involve creative expression in some way and in the main do not have a clear final outcome. The focus here is therefore both on data collection and also on exploration, understanding and meaning making.

## RESEARCH PHILOSOPHIES AND PARADIGMS

As mentioned in Chapter 1, it is important for researchers to locate their philosophical position and decide on their methodology. This is because different traditions affect the way data are collected, handed and interpreted. Although qualitative researchers have moved away from empiricism and rationalism as epistemological positions, they still draw from a different set of philosophical perspectives to drive their epistemological positions. While it may or may not be easy to identify a philosophical stance, knowing the impact of different methodologies is vital to the effective collection of data in terms of the research design, rigour, and subsequent presentation of the study. Coupled with needing to take up a philosophical position is also the need to take a personal stance. A personal stance is a position taken towards an issue that is derived from a person's beliefs and views about the world. It reflects deeply held attitudes and concerns about what is important.

In social research and in our work as educationalists, we are conscious of our identity and our position in relation to our colleagues and our students, although we sometimes leave this out of our research. It seems to us that it is a concept that is deeply embedded in both our perceptions of self and our perspectives of the world, which ultimately is connected to our personal stance. Our use of the term, personal stance, follows Salmon:

Taking the metaphor of personal stance gives a different meaning, not just to learning, but also to teaching, which, as teachers, we think about less often than we should. Because personal stance refers to the positions which each of us takes up in life, this metaphor emphasises aspects of experience which go deeper than the merely cognitive, and which reflect its essentially relational, social and agentic character (Salmon, 1989: 231)

Our stances are as educationalists, educational researchers, supervisors, spouses, parents, runners and innovation consultants who spend our time managing these often-colliding worlds. As researchers and supervisors we often seek to enable people to reach their desired potential, yet the notion of 'helping' gets clouded by conflicting notions of self-direction and autonomy and the relationship between facilitation and intransigent institutional requirements. What all these issues have in common is recognising the influence of our personal stances on the people and contexts in which we work and learn. Having taken a philosophical position and recognized our personal stance, it is important to locate these in relation to the methodology adopted.

---

### *Reflection*

As researchers it is important that our personal stance matches, wherever possible, with a methodology. Whilst some researchers suggest that the most important issue is a match between what is being studied and the methodology, in arts-related research we suggest that personal stance also holds sway. This is because it is difficult to undertake research in, for example, grounded theory, when our personal stance stands against the belief that theory can actually be grounded.

---

## WHAT IS THE RELATIONSHIP BEWEEN METHODOLOGY AND METHODS?

Research methodology is defined here as the approach to research adopted that is based on a philosophical position and which is guided initially by the research question. Methodology informs the way in which data are collected, managed, analysed and interpreted; it is central to the way participants are seen and the nature of truth(s) within the study. In much qualitative research it is possible to see methodology as a lens. However, in arts-related research there tend to be more overlaps between data collection and data interpretation than in other forms of qualitative inquiry. For example Savin-Baden and Major (2013) suggest this lens:

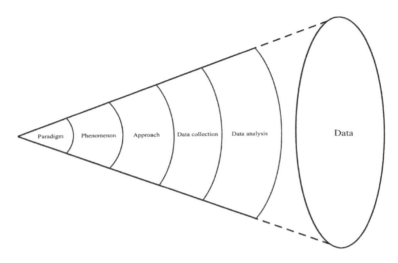

*Figure 4.1. Qualitative research lens*

However, in arts-related research we suggest that this lens is more fluid, as follows:

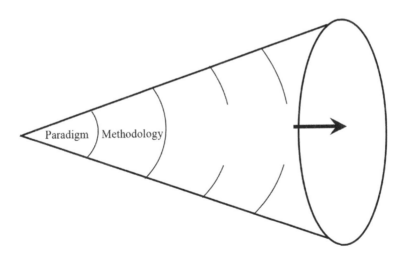

*Figure 4.2. Qualitative research lens for arts-related research*

Despite such fluidity, it is still vital to have an underpinning paradigm and methodology. This is because we believe it is important to understand the impact of people's perspectives as well as their contexts, in order that we can recognise how we have situated ourselves in relation to them. This is not meant to be a formula for locating our positioned identity in terms of race, gender or class, but instead to help us to consider as researchers:

– How is the research being undertaken, for whom, and with whom?
– What are the power relations and dynamics?
– How are data managed and interpreted, and who makes these decisions?
– How are people presented, represented, and located in the presentation of the study?

In order to deal with these issues, arts-related researchers need to have a clear understanding of methodology and methods in order to locate themselves and their study plausibly.

> *Methodology* — This is the particular type of qualitative research study undertaken, such as ethnography or phenomenology. Some researchers call these approaches research strategies, research designs, or research traditions.
>
> *Methods* — We define methods as the particular steps or processes taken during a study, such as interviewing or photovoice.
>
> *Arts-based methods* — These are the practices used to collect data that are often particular to arts-related studies, such as collage, photography or story telling.

Some academics and researchers suggest:

> … that to appreciate how visual arts contributes to human understanding, there is a need to locate artistic research within the theories and practices that surround art making. It is from this central site of creative practice that other forms of inquiry emerge, such as critical and philosophical analysis, historical and cultural commentary, and educational experience. This notion is a far cry from the stereotype that sees art experience as a warm, fuzzy, and essentially private matter. Rather, it affirms that artistic thinking and making are cognitive processes … (Sullivan, 2010: 97)

However, we argue that this somewhat utopian position suggests that artistic research and art making can be located outside philosophies and traditions that have been debated and discussed for decades. What is important we suggest is that those using arts-related approaches, of whatever kind, can locate their studies in, and in relation to, the following philosophical positions:

*Critical theory* — Critical theorists argue that some societal groups are privileged over others and that oppression is widespread and varied. Thus they seek to understand the ideologies that inform and affect both their research and their own stances, in an effort to gain knowledge. Simultaneously they strive to reduce systems of domination and increase autonomy of research participants. The critical social theorist view of reality is related to the influences of power and authority, as well as to how political, historical and socio-economic forces influence the people.

*Pragmatism* — Pragmatism is a philosophical tradition which asserts that truth may be interpreted in terms of the practical effects of what is believed and in particular the usefulness of these effects. The underlying idea is that the truth of an idea is dependent upon its workability; ideas or principles are true in so far as they work. For the pragmatist, reality is a process or an experience.

*Phenomenology* — Phenomenologists see reality as a product of the mind, so that meaning is shaped through individual experiences of the world. Thus understanding is necessarily biased because it is grounded in individual perceptions, an event or experience and because of the researcher's experience of history and traditions.

*Post-modern theory and post-structuralism* — Post-modern researchers and post-structuralists believe that there is no unified reality, but rather multiple and individual realities. Researchers in this area are concerned with power structures and hegemonies and how they maintain structures and enforce hierarchy, whilst striving to remain open to the attitudes, beliefs and values of participants.

*Constructionism* — Constructionists believe that hidden or private phenomena such as emotions gain their meaning through social settings and practice, and are therefore socially constructed. Reality is not entirely external and independent of individual conceptions of the world, and therefore signs and systems play an important part in the social construction of reality as individuals make and experience meaning together. However, social construction has led to a shift in thinking about the constructed nature of knowledge. Thus these researchers suggest that, instead of focusing on the mind (the cognitive approach), it is important to recognise that the world is shared; the world is produced and understood through interchanges between people and shared objects and activities.

*Constructivism* — Constructivism is based upon the notion that reality is a product of one's own creation so that reality cannot be separated from knowledge of it. Thus subjectivity and objectivity are in a sense united. The result is that these researchers believe that the only thing that they may come to know is people's constructions of their own realities. Therefore research emphasises gaining data concerning how individuals construct knowledge.

The idea of taking a philosophical position may be new to many researchers and particularly those involved in arts-related research. Furthermore, locating ourselves in relation to the study is challenging, because our perspectives change and move through the research and as our lives and context shift. Thus there is a need for constant reflexive interpretation in relation to the data we have collected, as well as at different stages of the research process.

At times it can be easier to ignore our stances, views and circumstances and the ways they can have an impact on data, and instead act as if we are outside the situation looking in. However, it is additionally important both to understand our philosophical position, stance and the methodology we have adopted, and also the types of data that might be collected and the methods used to collect them, as Lynn Butler Kisber, MGill University, Canada explains below:

---

**Author Reflection**
*Arts-based Qualitative Research*[1]
**Lynn Butler Kisber,** MGill University, Canada

Previously, I have suggested that a helpful way to classify qualitative research is to examine the processes researchers use to make meaning of the phenomena which they are studying (Butler-Kisber, 2010). After a careful examination of a vast array of qualitative work, it became apparent to me that meaning-making processes take three basic forms, thematic, narrative, and artistic. These are not mutually exclusive, and they are often used in combination with each other to produce more nuanced understandings (Boyle, 2011; Furlini, 2005; Maxwell and Miller, 2008; Mesher, 2006; Arora, 2013), and there is also a good deal of variation within each of these categories. Thematic approaches to meaning making, in which research material is unitized, coded and then reconstructed into large, conceptual themes, strip away the context, but allow the researcher to find commonalities across individuals/cases. Narrative approaches retain the contiguity and context of the information and make connections within and among the research material, in order to give a deep and holistic understanding of a particular phenomenon or experience (Barone, 1983; Dunlop, 2000; Steeves, 2000). Artistic approaches evoke emotion and metaphoric meaning, and reveal unspoken and unintentional understandings that otherwise may remain hidden (Butler-Kisber, 2008; Davis and Butler-Kisber, 1999; Markus, 2007).

The roots of these meaning-making approaches come from many different traditions and voices, but most often are attributed to particular researchers and theorists who helped to create spaces and support for doing a particular type of this work. Thematic meaning making has a long history and emanated from the work in grounded theory by sociologists Glaser and Strauss (1967). Narrative

---

*Continued*

representation of research has been the hallmark of qualitative research for decades, but it was Bruner (1986) who built on the work of Sassure and posited that human thought is guided by two distinct thought processes, the narrative and paradigmatic or logico-scientific modes (Maxwell and Miller, 2008, p.463).

Narrative thinking processes organize thoughts temporally, while paradigmatic thought processes organize information conceptually. The recognition that narrative thinking was a distinct way of understanding came from the work of feminist researchers, who disrupted mainstream thinking by including participant voices and marginalized stories. The work of educational researchers such as Barone (1989), Elbaz (1983), Clandinin and Connelly (2000), and Lawrence-Lightfoot (1983) among others, helped to validate and propagate these narrative forms of meaning making.

Narrative work is perhaps the chronological and methodological bridge between thematic and arts-based research. Arts-based work takes many forms (poetic, visual, and performative) and includes the various subcategories or strands of these forms.

Arts-based research is about opening up peripheral spaces for new understandings and embodied ways of thinking in the search for socially just and equitable practices (Savin-Baden & Major, 2013). History is replete with many instances of artists using their works to challenge the social fabric, and of researchers, in anthropology and elsewhere, who have incorporated artistic practices into their studies. It was Eisner (1991) and McNiff (1998) however, who suggested the parallels between work of both artists and qualitative researchers. This initiated important conversations across many fields. It ignited wide-spread interest, and validated the potential and accessibility of this kind of work. Also, it gave permission to researchers to venture into this territory; those researchers who had the background or the propensities for doing arts-based work, but had kept these skills separate from their research, or simply repressed them. Artistic meaning making is used for researcher reflexivity, for eliciting responses or producing new interpretations among participants, and/or for representing the research. The permutations and combinations that are possible in arts-based work make it both exciting and accessible (Savin-Baden & Major, 2013).

In the last decade, there has been an increasing acceptance of arts-based work as shown by research conferences, dissertations, and journal publications. There is no doubt that arts-based research has been facilitated by digital technology and the visual and aural opportunities it provides for both producing and disseminating the work. It is because of the increasing interest in and possibilities for arts-based research, that there are many requests from graduate students for guidance and instruction for producing high-quality research. To date, however, there remains a lack of attention given to arts-based research in graduate curricula, and few efforts to institutionalize it. When there is a small core of arts-based researchers at an institution, this seems to help, but without this, faculty members and students frequently feel isolated and

*Continued*

marginalized. As well, arts-based researchers have difficulty finding the expertise to assist them in developing the necessary technical and aesthetic skills for doing this kind of work. Arts-based research needs to be able to withstand the criticism directed at it from those with different epistemological perspectives.

This can be done best by avoiding less than stellar work, and by providing sufficient explication and transparency to be credible. It is more difficult to do this in the arts because of the intuitive and idiosyncratic nature of artistic processes. Transparency enhances the rigour of the research, and equally importantly helps to contribute in building a repertoire of methodological possibilities for other researchers in the various arts-based strands. The eclectic quality of arts-based work makes it interesting and engaging, but researchers need to take responsibility for ensuring transparency is a high priority.

There have been many excellent efforts to set up criteria for evaluating arts-based research (Bamford, 2005; Barone & Eisner, 1997; Finley, 2003; Kerry-Moran, 2008; Knowles & Cole, 2008; Piirto, 2002; Richardson, 2000; Sullivan, 2009), which build upon, elaborate, or contest criteria for ensuring quality in qualitative research generally. There is not yet, however, a consensus about what should count as quality in arts-based research, and why. Part of this is because there are those who believe that one must have a background in a particular art(s) to venture into the arts-based arena. There are others who feel strongly that this is a form of elitism that post-modernism has tried to overturn (Butler-Kisber, 2010), and that this research world should be open to anyone. I suggest another reason, and one that has not received enough attention. It is the many differences that exist among the various strands of arts-based work that make it so difficult to generate these criteria. Although there may be some agreement about some basic qualities that can apply to all arts-based research, evaluating poetry, for example, is in many ways quite different from evaluating a visual form of research.

There is no turning back from arts-based research now. Only a decade or so ago, arts-based work was considered alternative, while now it has established a spot in mainstream conferences and journals. There are, however, forces such as the standards movement, and conservative policies held by granting agencies, which can rein in the gains that have been made to date. Perhaps the digital world having opened up immense possibilities, which will surely increase as technology advances, will help to mitigate these forces. In the meantime, I believe there are some very practical and positive things that arts-based researchers could be doing.

First, an effort should be made to survey researchers to generate an annotated list of exemplary arts-based dissertations from around the world. This 'digital repository' would be most helpful to other researchers and their graduate students. Second, spaces should be created at conferences, and in other contexts, where artists and researchers can dialogue and ultimately agree upon some criteria for

*Continued*

evaluating the various strands of arts-based work. Finally, I believe it would be most helpful and interesting to establish regional lists of arts-based researchers indicating the arts-based strand(s) of work, the institutional affiliation, and point of contact. This would serve to validate the arts-based research community, provide a sense of the scope of the work, and help to build collaborative research possibilities across countries and beyond.

*Cole and Knowles (2008, p. 59), suggest that arts-informed work, "is research in the social sciences that is influenced by, but not based in, the arts broadly conceived." As an educational researcher that came to the arts, I have tended to use this term. For this article, however, I am using the term "arts-based" as it seems to be more universally accepted.

## WHAT ARE METHODS AND WHAT ARE DATA?

Methods are the particular steps or processes taken during a study, such as interviewing or photovoice; they are the mechanism and process through which data are collected. However, in the context of arts-related research, data is, in the main, more complicated and less bounded than in other forms of qualitative research. This is because data collection, data analysis and data interpretation, as well as data representation can overlap and merge. However, at the outset, having a sense of the kinds of data to be collected and how this might be undertaken is important and we underline some of the methods here:

### Interviews

There are articles and tomes about interviewing, types of interviews and interviewing techniques. Hollway and Jefferson (2000) have suggested that four principles facilitate the production of the interviewee's meaning, which we have adapted here:

1. Use open-ended questions: 'Tell me about your stories of being a doctor'
2. Elicit stories: 'Relate examples of learning in fieldwork that are particularly memorable.'
3. Avoid 'why' questions—these tend to encourage intellectualization and can be threatening
4. Follow up using respondents' ordering and phrasing: 'You said working in a different environment was very complicated, can you tell me some more about that?'

We suggest in arts-related research that it is best to use open approaches such as semi-structured or unstructured interviews. However, it is important to note that data can also be captured within interview settings in ways that are not necessarily verbal. Thus the participant might respond to a question by expressing their perspective through a pose, a poem or a dance.

*Semi structured interview* — In a semi-structured interview, the researcher asks predefined questions (usually 12-15 are sufficient for a one hour interview) and then also uses additional questions to follow up a participant's response, in order to elicit greater detail. The usual strategy is to begin with broad general questions and to narrow the focus as the interview progresses. The questions need to be open-ended enough to allow interviewees to express their perspectives on a topic or issue, whilst also enabling a degree of comparison across respondents.

*Unstructured* — An unstructured interview relies upon the spontaneous generation of questions which tend to arise from the context as well as the focus of the research study. As a result questions tend to be broad and open-ended, that elicit wide-ranging responses. The strength of this kind of approach is that it allows the interviewer to test preliminary understandings, while remaining highly responsive.

*Focus group interviews* — A focus group interview is a form of group interview, but the primary difference between it and other group interviews is that interaction of the group members is encouraged. Focus group interviews can allow the researcher to view social processes in action.

*Focus Groups*

A focus group is a gathering of a limited number of individuals, who through conversation with each other. provide information about a specific topic, issue or subject. Focus groups originated in the area of marketing in America during the early 1920s, although it was not until the 1960s that focus groups became popular for collecting feedback in advertising. Focus groups are used to provide quick information about specified members' opinions. Two particular types are useful in arts-related research:

*Delphi technique* — The Delphi technique is a focus group method that is usually used to gain consensus on a particular issue and is used for gathering data from participants within their domain of expertise. The researcher undertakes 3-4 rounds of open ended interview questions over a few months, in order to gain convergence of opinion on an issue and correlate informed judgement, as well as exposing assumptions that may not be discovered through survey questionnaires and interviews.

*Nominal group technique* — This approach comprises structured small group discussion and was originally developed by Delbecq and VandeVen (1971). This technique prevents the discussion being dominated by one person whilst at the same time encourages passive members to engage and speak out. At the end of the discussion people vote and a set of solutions and recommendations are compiled. The advantage with this approach is that voting is anonymous so participation in the decision making is equal, yet this can also result in a lack of convergence of opinion resulting in disparate responses and results, as well as a sense that the process has been formal and mechanical.

## Performance Ethnography and Ethnodrama

Performance ethnography is a broad descriptor for a number of performative methods used by qualitative researchers. It was developed originally to examine the political nature of practice by Conquergood (2002), who argued that performance should be seen as stories 'to open the space between analysis and action . . . and to pull the pin on the binary opposition between theory and practice.' (2002: 145). Ethnotheater involves a particular dramatic staging of social research. Ethnodrama is an approach developed and drawn from 'ethnography' and 'drama,' coined by the anthropologist Turner (Turner 1982: 100). Ethnodrama is used when researchers believe that dramatic art form is the best way to both research and represent something that is an exploration of the human condition. We suggest there is strong overlap and overplay between ethnotheater and ethnodrama. Perhaps the best explanation of both is provided by Saldaña:

Ethnotheatre consists of 'the traditional craft and artistic techniques of theatre production to mount for an audience a live performance event of research participants' experiences and/or the researcher's interpretations of data'

Ethnodrama consists of 'dramatized, significant selections of narrative collected through interviews, participant observation, field notes, journal entries, and/or print and media artifacts such as diaries, television broadcasts, newspaper articles, and court proceedings.' (Saldaña 2005: 1-2)

In practice this approach to data collection involves writing and presenting monologues and dialogues, and the scripted adaptation and dramatisation of qualitative studies.

## Installations

Installations tend to overlap with other data collection methods such as photography, art and digital approaches. As mentioned in Chapter 1 Harrison (2013) created a circus tent as a means of presenting his data. He adopted auto ethnography to interpret and examine his own story created through self portraits.

Installations can vary considerably. Static and situated pieces that resemble traditional artwork can be created, and then data collected as a response to the work. Other forms of installations are those where the participant becomes a part of the installation – which is particularly the case in digital installations such as those undertaken by Upton (2012), who uses Second Life as a means of creating innovative digital spaces in public spheres. Such interactive art installations are often placed in public spaces and thus data collected can be overt or covert.

*Sequential Art*

This is the art of comic books and graphic novels, the panels of images, text boxes and word balloons put side by side, in order to tell some kind of narrative. Weaver-Hightower (2010) suggests that what is central to understanding sequential art is closure, through firstly recognizing the images on the pages, such as the lines and printed dots, as if they were objects. The second way that sequential art relies on closure — and unique to it over other representational art forms like photographs or paintings — is from panel to panel. However, the sense in which sequential art can be a research method is that it can be used as a means of collecting data, as well as for analysis and presentation. Weaver-Hightower explains the creation of the panel overleaf:

---

**Author Reflection**
*Sequential Art*
**Marcus Weaver-Hightower**, University of North Dakota, USA

It depicts a short sequence of around sixty seconds taken from a pilot project I did a few years ago that looked at how students would regard the presence of an operator-less camera in their classroom. A young man, who I have given the pseudonym "Phillip," is working with his group to plan a field trip. Or at least he's supposed to be working on that. Instead, he is talking with his groupmate about something unrelated, and he is breaking numerous classroom and school rules by eating in class, violating the dress code, and--because this is an English class--not using Standard English grammar. The transcript depicts the teacher's multiple attempts to get Phillip to submit to her will through several overlapping sanctions she tries to apply. Phillip, as we can see, gets the last laugh because the videocamera is there to capture his one last show of resistance, one that ultimately the teacher will see later but that, importantly, preserves his ability to stay in the class at that moment (e.g., Giroux, 1983). Originally, this was typed up as a relatively standard text transcript but the transcript made it very hard to show, in words, what was actually happening. Much of the flavour of the scene was lost in converting it into social scientific text. When the scene is converted into sequential art, though, a whole set of new analytic choices are available, choices that make comic panels a powerful tool for qualitative research.

---

*Figure 4.3. Sequential art*

## Collage

Collage is an arts-based research approach to meaning-making through the juxtaposition of a variety of pictures, artefacts, natural objects, words, phrases, textiles, sounds, and stories.

Bead collage, for example, is a method that invites participants to reflect, communicate and construct their experience through their manipulation of beads and other objects. Kay (2013) explained how she used beads to collect data for her interviews which were used as both data collection and data representation:

> I brought materials to the interview that were similar to those I used in my own art and art therapy practice. I arranged tins and baskets with stones, crystals, antique/ recycled jewelry, handmade beads, and miscellaneous found objects (buttons, keys, nuts, bolts, seeds, stones, clips) on a table in each art teacher's respective classroom where the interviews took place (Kay, 2013)

57

Collage is not meant to provide one-to-one transfer of information; rather, it strives to create metaphoric evocative texts through which readers, audiences, and patrons create their own meanings on a given research topic. Usually, material is taken out of context from a range of sources and used to create a new assemblage from the bricolage collected. What underpins the creation of research collages is the attempt to construct meanings about the research question and process, the participants, and emerging themes.

### Photography

Traditionally, visual methods such as photography have been used as providing illustrations to the text without actual analysis of the photographs (Banks, 2000: 11). Nevertheless an example of using photographs as data collection is provided by Holm (2008), who explains:

> In the doctoral level qualitative research methods class in this study, the professor taught about the use of visual research methods by giving the students the task of taking photographs of what it meant to be a doctoral student. Hence, in this study, it was explicitly the students' perceived reality, their own construction of their identity as a doctoral student that was of interest (Holm: 2008)

However, in the last two decades there has been increasing interest in the use of photographs as data. There are a number of different approaches and a few of these are presented below:

*Visual ethnography* — Visual ethnography involves studying phenomena using visual media such as photography, sketches, maps and video whilst also investigating cultural objects and artifacts that are visual representations with embedded meanings, or that have an impact on everyday life because of their visual presence. Pink (2001) has argued for this approach, and suggests that visual material offers a variety of meaning to the audience:

> [T]here are no fixed criteria that determine which photographs are ethnographic. Any photograph may have ethnographic interest, significance or meanings at a particular time or for a specific reason. The meanings of photographs are arbitrary and subjective; they depend on who is looking. The same photographic image may have a variety of (perhaps conflicting) meanings invested in it at different stages of ethnographic research and representation, as it is viewed by different eyes and audiences in diverse temporal historical, spatial, and cultural contexts. (p. 51)

Ethnography is an approach focusing in depth on a particular context or group of people. It invariably involves researchers taking themselves away from their own routines of everyday life, in order to observe and study other cultures and settings. However, one of the central challenges of this approach is the positioning of ethnography, since there are a variety of types and it is not entirely clear in visual ethnography which types are being adopted. Ethnography can range from post-positivist approaches such as realist ethnography through to constructionist approaches such as duo and auto ethnography. In adopting this method it will be important for a researcher to be clear about their ethnographic stance.

*Documentary photography* — This refers to photography used to chronicle significant and historical events and it generally focuses on a single topic or story in-depth over time. Researchers adopting this approach to data collection spend time working with participants to build trust and strong relationships, are open and clear about their intentions, and are ready to have their assumptions challenged.

---

### *Example*

Jacob Riis (1849-1914) was a police reporter for the New York Tribune newspaper. In the early 1880s, he supplemented his investigative reporting of the city's notorious Lower East Side slums with his own photographs (MCNY) and soon became known as one of the city's most important social reformers. An immigrant from Denmark to the United States in 1870, Riis, who originally trained to be a carpenter, published his first and most important book, How the Other Half Lives, in 1890. The catalyst for citywide reform of building codes and slumlord-tenant relations, the book continues to serve as a model for all photographers and urban historians dedicated to social change within the city.

Department of Photographs. 'Early Documentary Photography'. In Heilbrunn Timeline of Art History. New York: The Metropolitan Museum of Art, 2000 – http://www.metmuseum.org/toah/hg/edph/he_edph.htm (October 2004)

---

*Photo elicitation* — Photographs are also commonly used to elicit information in interviews and can be taken either by the researcher or by the participants themselves. The purpose of using photographs in interviews is not only to encourage the interviewee to tell about their everyday lives, remember past events or to unlock forgotten information, but also to reveal participants' hidden views and values. Photographs taken by the researcher tend to focus on aspects that the researcher has found interesting, incomprehensible or important in some way. The images are the most important and decisive element of the investigation. They define the problem, describe the context, provide and interpret the data, argue a case for the findings and reveal conclusions (which, in turn, may also be photos). The photographs included in a visual arts educational project are combined to generate formal, narrative and conceptual interactions.

*Photovoice* — This approach involves the process of taking photography in conjunction with social action. For example, participants are asked to represent an issue, concern or express a view through the photograph. Researchers work with the individual and community to develop narratives through the photographs. Wang and Burris (1994) were the proponents of this approach and created 'photo novella' which now is more commonly known as photovoice, as a way to enable rural women of Yunnan Province, China, to influence the policies and programs that affected them. Wang and Burris (1994) argue that the method was influenced by the work of Freire (1970) and is now often used with community groups as a means of data collection, representation and community action.

*Storytelling*

Stories tend to have context, characters, plot, place, turning points and resolutions. Researchers examine and use these conventions when introducing the experiences of the participants and presenting their stories. Narrative approaches may use plots and characters in order to draw the reader into the story, and as Bruner argues, most narrative 'involves an Agent who Acts [character] to achieve a Goal [plot] in a recognisable Setting [context] by use of a certain Means [plot]' (Bruner 1996: 94). Bullough and Pinnegar (2001) make a distinction between *story* and *plot* in that they see a story as a sequence of events narrated in a linear, chronological order; a telling of events. A plot, on the other hand, is a sequence of events that are organised to engage the reader emotionally. Stories do not always have a plot or structured storyline, but are often interruptions or reflections of a storied life. Storied lives may have unplanned interruptions such as an unexpected illness that may disrupt identities, thus changing the story and the storied-ness of lives. The stories are the means of understanding participants, since storytelling tends to be closer to actual life events than other methods of research that are just designed to elicit explanations. By focusing on gathering stories, data may be collected in a variety of ways, including stories, journals, field notes, letters, conversations, interviews, family stories, photos (and other artefacts) and life experiences.

*Listening and Action Spaces*

Lorenzo (2010) used listening and action spaces as a means of collecting data in the context of narrative action reflection workshops, as both a research method and strategy for social change. The project sought to explore how disabled women living in poor communities could equalize opportunities for human development and social change. In practice the spaces were created through workshops and incorporated the use of storytelling and creative activities as data triggers. Telling and listening to stories enables researchers and participants to discover the emotions and meanings of human actions, in order to begin social and political change. In practice this is undertaken in 4 phases:

Phase 1 is about *Setting the Scene*. It starts with an initial storytelling group of no more than 8-10 participants so that they are not rushed in sharing their stories.

Phase 2 is about *Action Planning*, comprising a reflective process to examine the telling of their stories, and what may have occurred as a result of telling and listening to stories.

Phase 3 is gathering data of collective experiences as well as being a strategy for change.

Phase 4 involves dissemination so that the workshops produce both benefits and outcomes during the research process. Lorenzo argues:

> Listening spaces allow multiple voices around different themes to emerge, which then enable participants to identify possible actions over time, so that a network of listening and action spaces is created, leading to collective action. (Lorenzo, 2010: 142)

## *Reflective Writing*

Reflective writing is often just seen as part of the researcher's field notes and undervalued as data. Field notes comprise a record of behaviour, events and surroundings of the research site. Field notes typically contain a date, time, location and details of what or who is being observed. Reflection is predominantly spoken about in terms of a sense making process and tends to be seen as the researcher:

- Thinking about experiences and ideas so as to discover new connections or conclusions to guide future action.
- Self-appraisal of what is currently occurring, to try to glean a new or different perspective.
- Evaluating and critiquing action – theirs or someone else's.
- Searching their understanding to bring meaning to the surface.
- Searching and self-discovering by other forms of reflection

Thus the beginning of writing for many researchers originates in understanding how to position themselves within the academic community, of developing a location, a space and a stance from which to write. Writing tends to begin with our narrative view of other peoples' work, our perspectives on academic life, and often our values and beliefs about what is important in academe. Thus to adopt it for research and as a method for data collection is often initially troublesome. Furthermore, what is recorded is driven by research questions. However, Armitage and Welsby (2009) argue that writing arts-based inquiry is inviting the audience to participate in art with the researcher. Moon, drawing on Hatton and Smith (1995), suggests using these different forms of writing, which we believe can be used for data collections:

> *Descriptive writing* — This is a description of events or literature reports. There is no discussion beyond description. This writing is considered not to show evidence of reflection. It is important to acknowledge that some parts of

a reflective account will need to describe the context – but in this case, writing does not go beyond description.

*Descriptive reflection* — There is basically a description of events, but the account shows some evidence of deeper consideration in relatively descriptive language. There is no real evidence of the notion of alternative viewpoints in use.

*Dialogic reflection* — This writing suggests that there is a 'stepping back' from the events and actions which leads to a different level of discourse. There is a sense of 'mulling about', discourse with self and an exploration of the role of self in events and actions. There is consideration of the qualities of judgements and of possible alternatives for explaining and hypothesising. The reflection is analytical or integrative, linking factors and perspectives.

*Critical reflection* — This form of reflection, in addition to dialogic reflection, shows evidence that the learner is aware that the same actions and events may be seen in different contexts with different explanations associated with the contexts. They are influenced by 'multiple historical and socio-political contexts', for example. (Moon, 2001)

Authors may choose to juxtapose image and text, use metaphor or experiment with other non-traditional reporting formats. Arts-based writing tends to be highly creative both in style and format. In this form, the researcher may choose not to assume the role of narrator but rather to let the art re-presentation speak for itself.

## CONCLUSION

This chapter has argued that in order to use arts-related research effectively it is vital for researchers to locate themselves philosophically and take a personal and methodological stance towards their research. By doing this, researchers will then be able to choose appropriate methods to collect data. This chapter has noted some of the many methods available for data collection for arts-related research, although there are many others available.

# ISSUES OF ANALYSIS, INTEPRETATION AND REPESENTATION

## *Rendering, Portrayal, and Praxis*

### INTRODUCTION

The challenges of undertaking arts-related research include managing the data collected and making the shift from analysis to interpretation. This process is often hidden from the reader or viewer and seen as something that is a private or covert process. Indeed to consider analysis and interpretation as a predetermined set of instructions may feel counter-intuitive to arts-related researchers; an unwanted process which seeks to contain and place boundaries on practices which are expected to be open and spontaneous. Yet we suggest that in working out, investigating and theorizing how to proceed with arts-related research, a conscious awareness of, and sharing of practice is necessary in order to defend one's work. We also appreciate that traditional methods of qualitative analysis cannot be applied easily, and that the use of appropriate language and a consideration of process is required, in order to help denote what is being done differently in arts-related research. In this chapter we consider analysis, interpretation and representation, along with other arts-related terms such as rendering, portrayal and praxis. We delineate a number of approaches for undertaking analysis, interpretation and representation, which are offered as a means of supporting researchers new to the field, as well as ensuring that arts-related research can do justice to those involved.

### ANALYSIS AND INTERPRETATION

As noted earlier in Chapter 4, data collection, analysis and interpretation in arts-related research may be viewed as simultaneous acts of revelation and illumination, through the process of unravelling, reordering and restructuring data and process, in order to examine what has occurred, or is occurring. The inquiry may be dealing with abstract forms of representation and traditional methods may be displaced by innovative and interactive ones; therefore the artist researcher might, as Hockney (2008) suggests, 'ask questions and make theories afterwards'.

63

Analysis in arts-related research may therefore challenge the typical gathering and interpretation of data as understood by social science researchers trained in qualitative traditions, where inductive approaches are used as the researcher makes sense of units of data to uncover a larger picture (Savin-Baden & Major, 2012). Whilst many qualitative approaches use methods to explore phenomena and reveal meaning, arts-related research is more interested in 'acts of theorizing as complication' (Irwin & Springgay, 2008: 109). Meaning making is seen as plotting out a course of action as critical, reflective and investigative praxis (Stewart, 2008:124). As Sullivan argues:

> Analysis and interpretation need to be systematic and rigorous, but also inventive so as to reveal the rich complexity of the imaginative intellect as it is encountered and enacted within individual, social and cultural settings. (Sullivan, 2006:20)

Analysis and interpretation then, in arts-related research, are used to embrace the relationships between the data (the experience of the phenomena), knowing (theory), doing (praxis) *and* making (aesthetic creativity). Understanding experience through theory, praxis and making thus provides opportunities to uncover knowledge between theory, practice and creative activity, and allows each to impact on the other (Irwin & Springgay, 2008: 110). Further, the importance of what happens in the spaces in between what is known, and yet to be named, requires the researcher to constantly question and engage with the messiness or complexity inherent in relationships between thoughts and actions, subjects, art forms and contexts.

Whilst messiness and complexity is inherent within arts-related analysis, we suggest it is nonetheless important to be mindful of how the researcher undertakes this process and generates learning (findings) from the 'event'. Arts-related researchers may draw on methods of analysis such as ethnographic research (for example, semiotic analysis), phenomenology (interpretive phenomenological analysis) or narrative inquiry (narrative analysis). The methodology used will influence the focus of the analysis and therefore the findings. For example, in narrative analysis the researcher will focus on the ways in which participants have shared stories to explore, examine and reflect on their experiences, with the story being viewed as the 'social product' that individuals use to share unique experiences (Savin-Baden & Major, 2012). In semiotic analysis, the symbolic nature of signs and symbols that are present in the data are examined, by exploring how meanings are derived from the relationships between the sign or the symbol, the cultural references associated with the sign, and how that has been defined and given meaning culturally (Berger, 1998). Use of such analytical methods may be useful on their own, or we propose, may provide an important starting point, as they may be inadequate in capturing the complexity of the arts-related data. Creating a rich picture of events requires aesthetic considerations as well. We suggest then, that there is justification for use of an extended language and practice which can clearly denote 'arts-related narrative analyses or 'arts-related thematic analyses'.

Analysis and interpretation in arts-related research are not modelled on predictive processes; rather, 'understandings emerge from the associative relations among complex interactions' (Sumara & Carson, 1997: xviii). Thus relationships between the data, the arts-related researcher, the research team and research participants, the audience, theory, and the cultural, economic and political settings are all components of the analytic process (relative to the theoretical underpinning and methodological choices made). This bringing together of the self and other, inside and outside influences, as a way of engaging in the analytical process is illustrated in Figure 5.1. This process captures how arts-related research involves

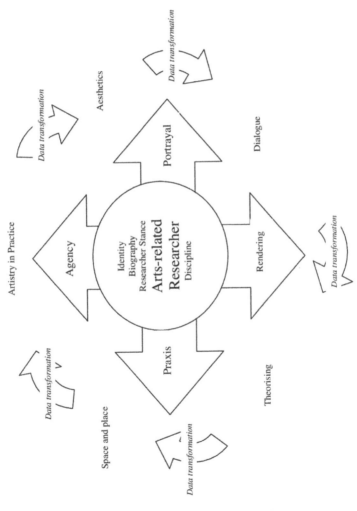

*Figure 5.1. A model of rendering, portrayal and praxis*

creative action with others and materials, critical reflection, translation and depiction, whilst remaining mindful of discourses and contexts which are used to frame the production and interpretation of the research findings. The researcher is required to make uncertain moves above and beyond documented practices, which are challenging but necessary conditions for analytical work that is 'on the move' (Jackson & Mazzei, 2011). Jackson and Mazzei suggest that in the analytical process, the researcher and the researched are both subject to change, as is the audience or viewer, so that as the research data become transformed and offer something else, something new is made available; a new portrayal, a re-presentation of the phenomena (Irwin & Springgay, 2008).

## THE MODEL OF RENDERING, PORTRAYAL, AND PRAXIS

This process model, as illustrated above, presents the many factors which are combined in the data analysis and interpretation process, each aspect informing the other whilst also coming together to represent 'the whole'; the (new) aesthetic work. It offers conceptual clarity when sharing the analytical process of data transformation with others. Each aspect of the model is considered in detail below, starting with a focus on the arts-related researcher.

### Arts-related Researcher

In the analytical process the arts-related researcher is a central figure in shaping the inquiry, especially if the researcher is an artist thinking and working within their particular medium. The arts-related researcher's biography, identity, researcher stance, discipline and worldview are all brought to bear on how they think, respond, problem solve and create. This is illustrated in Figure 5.2. The examination of the personal and the professional emerges through reflexivity and may include incorporating data found in the researcher's reflective diary notes, selection of artefacts, narratives and other forms of creative expression revealed during the inquiry, which acknowledges the relationships between the phenomenon under study alongside a personal critical examination of the data through the art form(s) selected.

### Agency

Drawing on the work of Giddens (1984), agency is defined as being able to act or to intervene in the world, whilst recognising the influence of social structure and social actions which inform, and are reproduced in what people do. Thus agency in the analytical act is inextricably linked to researchers' decision-making in the creative process, as they work to decipher, translate, uncover, make judgments and envision relationships amongst concepts and data sets, artistic genres and art forms. The

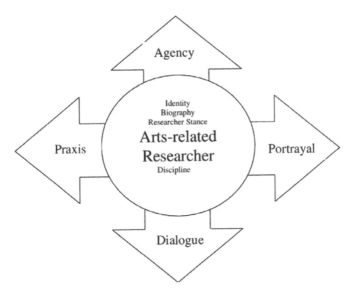

*Figure 5.2. Analysis and interpretation and the arts-related researcher*

relationships between the researcher, participants, audiences, social systems and the powerfulness of practice culture are also of importance here, for example, in arts-engaging or arts-informing inquiry, where analysis or meaning making is a shared task.

Further, agency is linked to the researcher's reflexive beliefs about their own biography (Giddens, 1991); the arts-related researcher draws on insights from lived experience in order to decipher, translate, and create. Reflexivity and reflection are therefore crucial parts of agency within the analytical process and are located within the creative practice itself, in the relationships between the researcher, the participants, the phenomena and the art forms, which serve to prompt questions, issues, and decisions as responses occur and learning is experienced (Dewey, 1933).

*Praxis*

Praxis is derived from the Greek word '*prattein*', which literally translates as 'doing', and is defined here as the process in which the arts-related researcher translates their skill and disciplinary knowledge into practice through experimentation and the practicing of ideas through action, reflection and transformation (Friere, 1970). Sullivan identifies with arts-related research as:

[P]raxis of human engagement, yielding outcomes that can be individually liberating  and culturally enlightening (2004:74)

By considering the nature of the inquiry as fluid, as both personal and public, shifting and becoming, through reflection and action, praxis is possible. Praxis is present in the analytical process through the potential of art to 'change habits of expression; to provide for openness in the complexity of relations amongst things and people' (Carson & Sumara, 1997: xv). For example, when we come to explain what has happened, the 'so what', we are drawing on revelations and inference and shared meanings with others, complemented or challenged along with theory; a coming together of perspectives which are dynamic, and may be woven together, but are not fixed. Praxis in arts-related research therefore, is the relationships between the data, knowing or *theoria* (theory), creating or *poesis* (making) and doing, or *praxis*. It is about being present in the moment, drawing on experience and engaging aesthetically with meaning, self and other.

As a means of illustrating praxis in the critical and creative analytical process, Koro-Ljungberg's abstract from AERA (2013) captures her researcher focus on the importance of interrupting traditional analytical practices to enable praxis and new ways of learning, through her senses, experiences, discourses, images, and texts.

---

**Movement and Moments in Unthinkable Analysis**
**Presenter/Author**: Mirka E. Koro-Ljungberg (University of Florida)

**Scheduled Time:** Sun, April 28, 2013, 8.15 – 9.45 am Sir Francis Drake, Second Level - Carmel
**In Session**: Methodologies that move: Circus and celebration of Unthinkable Qualitative Inquiry

**Objective and significance**: Massumi (as cited in Rice, 2010) encouraged us to think about space that has the "ability to irrupt unexpectedly, to break out of or to break into the existing spatial grid, anywhere, at any moment" (p.34). This presentation will reach to that space by illustrating, discussing, and theorizing movements and example moments in unthinkable 'data analysis' during doctoral students' unpredictable interactions with data. In unthinkable 'analysis' researcher's lives, practices, emotions, and material experiences fold into each other in unexpected ways. Researchers take risks. Unthinkable 'data analysis' may include events and 'unreasonable' interactions with data that are generally systematically excluded from researchers' consciousness and acceptable academic discussions about research. Unthinkable 'data analysis' attempts to counter normativity and cultural dominance (see also Lemert, 2007). Furthermore, movements and moments in unthinkable 'data analysis' are situational and they hang together. Different worlds, people, data,

---

*Continued*

analytical tools, interpretations, practices, and settings come together in new, unpredictable and constantly changing ways in senses, experiences, discourses, images, and texts.

**Perspective**: The performances that I will share come from videos and visual examples from students, who interact with data in various ways as a response to the request from the instructor to 'analyze data in messy ways'. Stunts will illustrate how 'data analysis' that moves can lead to spontaneous connections, 'accident zones' and connectibility between different interactions with data. Additionally, students' stunts that describe their interactions with data have less to do with step-by-step approaches or direct application of documented procedures, and more with engaging, challenging, interesting, thought provoking, and sometimes pleasurable or threatening approaches to data and its various forms. Some stunts illustrate how analysis can be felt in its effects, with these being actualized through movement from one data sample to another, through analytical questions and responses folding on each other.

**Conclusion:** There is no clear, detached, objectified, purely technical or epistemologically smooth path to 'data analysis'. Derrida (1992) argued that responsibility begins with "the experience and experiment of the aporia. When the path is clear and given, when a certain knowledge opens up the way in advanced, the decision is already made, it might as well be said that there is none to make; irresponsibly" (p. 41). 'Data analysis' that takes risks and moves towards the unexpected can enable researchers to meet the other; other ways of knowing. These uncertain moves 'above and beyond' documented practices are challenging but necessary 'conditions' for methodological work that is unthinkable and always becoming. Unthinkable methodologies utilize the energies gained from conceptual hazard, unpredictability, ambiguity, and openness to the spontaneity as qualitative researchers relate their work to theories, epistemologies, and educational policies and practices.

*Portrayal*

Within the analytical act the use of art, poetry, dance and collage is part of the analysis process and the researcher's choice of art form and materials are, 'the tangible means that give form to imaginative thought' (Sullivan, 2006:31). Sullivan differentiates types of media within which the artist researcher may 'think' and create: for example, to think in a language (narrative forms, poetry), a context (spatial, community practice), and a medium (collage, music). By denoting such ways of thinking, expressive properties can be used to examine and represent the issue or concern which is being explored. In this way the medium and its form seek ways to express and open up possibilities for new meaning.

69

*Author Reflection*
**Katherine Wimpenny**

After presenting a research paper at AERA (2013) I was encouraged, by an artist-researcher, to develop an art practice as a regular type of theme. I was excited but also daunted somewhat by this proposition; I wasn't sure if I wanted to remain faithful to a particular art form, and if actually the choice of material or medium should be guided more by the research question or phenomena being explored. I would not seek to enforce a particular art form on participants, which may itself serve to silence voices. Yet as my thinking and practice has developed I can see how a regular type of art theme would be useful and advantageous for me to explore and experiment with, and so incorporate into my research practice. I have looked to others, such as Marcus Weaver-Hightower and his use of sequential art, (see Figure 5.3) which has defined his presence and expertise in the field, creating powerful impressions within which the artist-researcher explores and creates.

*Rendering*

The analytical portrayal process involves the researcher, and often the participants, in the act of 'rendering,' defined here as the translation of the data, through the creative act of depiction and interpretation of what is occurring. Thus rendering relates to interpreting the data into an artistic performance of some form. For example, the participant's narrative may be rendered into a painting or comic, with particular use of colour, shading, and texturing.

This section of the chapter has considered the model of rendering portrayal and praxis and the relationships concerning the art-related researcher. The following section identifies with a further layering of analytical relationships within which data transformation occurs. These comprise issues relating to person, context and practice, including artistry, space and place, aesthetics, theory and dialogue as identified in Figure 5.4 overleaf.

*Artistry in Practice*

Artistry in practice as an analytical task relates to the researcher's skill, knowledge and professional competency in coping effectively with situations of complexity and uncertainty (following Schön 1983; 1987). As the inquiry process unfolds, such practices reflect the researcher's epistemology of practice (professional and personal beliefs, values and opinions) that shape the way the researcher creates, experiments, uncovers, takes risks, critiques, interprets, acts and re-works the data. Artistry in practice includes how the researcher reflects-in-action and on-action, and how they collaborate

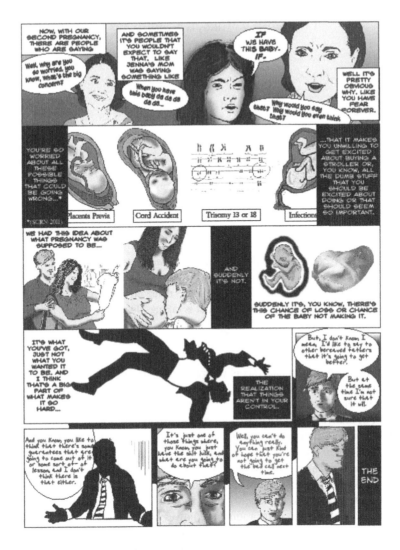

*Figure 5.3. An example of presenting research through comics by Marcus Weaver-Hightower, University of North Dakota, USA*

in meaning making with research participants and the audience. Good interaction skills are reflected by the researcher's demeanour, authenticity and respect towards participants. Building effective research relationships with participants is a pivotal component of artistry, and reflects the arts-related researcher's ability to recognise the subtleties and nuances of expression which occur in the inquiry process and through

71

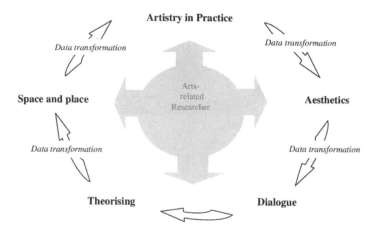

*Figure 5.4. Analysis, interpretation and the aesthetic context*

the handling of materials, as they encourage research participants to develop their relationship to, and understanding of, what is taking place with the art form.

*Aesthetics*

The aesthetic domain in analysis is where the artistic process and artistic 'products' are created. The aesthetic form used within the inquiry needs to be able to effectively capture the emotion, energy, themes and ideas which are revealed. Thus the aesthetic element of analysis involves decisions about artistic position or style, and with this the researcher's relationships to the art form. Arguably, the researcher needs to be proficient in their use of the chosen art, whether that is poetry, music, photography or theatre performance. Further, the more the researcher dedicates time to developing technical skills with the medium employed, the more aesthetically accomplished the work can be (Barone & Eisner, 2012). This does not mean that all researchers have to be capable of high end art production; however, dedication, experimentation and practice are recommended so that the aesthetic analysis effectively illuminates what is significant and revealing about the issue or concern being explored. Further, aesthetic decisions and 'products' should also be used in such a way so that the ideas are always partial, contestable and incomplete, rather than trying to reach an understanding and 'directly affect some facet of the world' (Barone & Eisner, 2012:53).

*Space and Place*

Space and place takes into account temporal as well as spatial concerns impacting upon the analysis process. This includes the notion of relational space, which draws on the idea of 'relational art', defined by art critic Bourriaud (2006) as, 'artistic practices which take as their theoretical and practical point of departure the whole of human relations and their social context, rather than an independent and private space'. As such the arts-related researcher may be viewed as a catalyst making use of space as a means of contextualising the inquiry within particular social-political-cultural contexts. For example, the audience may be called to a specific time and space where they can be active participants in the creation of meaning; a condition of 'relational aesthetics' (Irwin & Springgay, 2008: 114). Such analysis, for example drawing on a/r/tography, has potential to discover new meanings and possibilities in a relational space that is fluid and temporal, resulting in deep interactions within the inquiry (MacKenzie & Wolf, 2012; Irwin & de Cosson, 2004). For example, issues of context will influence the data analysis and interpretation process, not least when thinking about where and how the study findings will be disseminated. The 'work' may be located in a theatre space, or gallery, within a classroom, or within the pages of a poetry book. Spatial concerns then relate to the use of that space and how it is shaped by the moment or through past experiences. The work becomes space for 'potentiality'; a realm of possibility for human interaction, representing a social *interstice*, an independent and symbolic space (Bourriaud, 2006). Thus relational components are integral to making sense of the data and its aesthetic portrayal, placing emphasis upon the interaction between the researcher, context, aesthetics and audience.

In addition, experiencing something is often in the moment and can only be partially understood, rather than wholly reported (Aldridge, 2008). Thus the researcher supplies the 'conditions' for interaction in his or her work, whether painted, performed or written, to capture moments related to time and space. The task of the arts-related researcher is to analyze, rearrange and interpret the data as it has been experienced, to share the momentary observations, to present new insights and to create space for further questions to develop (MacKenzie & Wolf, 2012).

## Dialogue

Dialogue refers to conversations and relationships influencing responses to the research question and use of art form. It includes responses from participants and audience collaborations. As a 'living inquiry', arts-related research seeks to examine the complexity of relationships amongst researchers, artists, participants and communities, recognising the importance of how these roles and identities are conceptualised in the process of exploration. A commitment to learning with and through others offers a means of constructing greater meaning, through a communal approach focused on a wider, deeper interrogation of the data. This approach, when focused on a particular theme or area of study, enables the assumptions, and textured milieu of varying accounts to be exposed, described and explained in ways that bring new insights (Walsh & Downe, 2005). These 'openings' often signify contradiction and unease. Indeed, as Irwin and Springgay (2008: 113) suggest, the analytical and interpretive process is, 'to intentionally unsettle perception and complicate understanding'. Such ways of knowing may be offered to the audience who, in this case, are cast as interpreters. This dialogic process enables the arts-related researcher to reflect consciously on what is being learnt or uncovered, as well as turning that lens outward when considering the contribution of what other influences (people, space, theory) can reveal.

*Theorising*

Theorising is important within the analytical process as it provides, 'a rich contextual underbelly that can propel art inquiry' (Sullivan, 2006:31). Understanding the work of others, including textual critiques, can support analysis as well as provide contextualisation of the interpretations reached. Theorising can situate the analysis within a broader body of knowledge to complement or challenge understandings, informing new directions for arts-related research. As noted by Barone and Eisner (2012: 159), 'concepts without percepts are blind and percepts without concepts are empty.'

The influence of the methodology adopted is also an important component of theorising. For example, when analysing and interpreting narratives as part of storytelling, a heuristic method - RITES - as suggested by Leggo (2008: 6-7), may be used:

Step one: Read
The researcher reads the whole narrative to gain a general sense of the story.
Step two: Interrogate
The researcher asks some basic questions: who? what? where? when? why? how? So what?
Step three: Thematise
The researcher reads the narrative again with a focus on a theme, and spells out the parts of the story which relate to the theme.
Step four: Expand
The researcher expands on the theme by reflectively and imaginatively drawing connections and proposing possible meanings.
Step five: Summarise
The researcher summarises the theme in a general statement or two in order to indicate clearly what is learned from the narrative.

Similarly, Butler-Kisber and Poldama (2010) draw on constructivist perspectives in their use of collage as an interpretive tool, which they argue can reveal multiple ways of doing and understanding; naturally weaving together the practices of theory, praxis and doing.

Thus drawing on theory offers a way into meaning making, as well as making analytical leaps, which leads to theorising. Further, in arts-related research, theorising is not limited to propositions presented through narrative and the linguistic; rather communication takes place through a range of means – the visual, auditory and kinaesthetic, and casts its own understandings on the research subject. Arts-related inquiry can therefore be thought of as a 'theoretical enterprise' (Barone & Esiner, 2012); a complex range of art forms which can be used to promote knowing and understanding.

In summary, the 'model of rendering portrayal and praxis' presented here, provides a way of eliciting the complex processes involved in analysing multi-modal, multi-dimensional data. This final section of the chapter turns to how this process of analysis and interpretation relates to issues of representation.

## REPRESENTATION

Although representation is not easily disentangled from analysis and interpretation within the analytical process, it is important to consider how the findings from an inquiry can 'go public' and how best that might be communicated. Whilst conformity to funding requirements and reporting standards may be required, the central opportunity offered through arts-related research is through the aesthetic route, and enabling the reader or viewer to see what has been revealed during the inquiry process. For example, Cancienne (2008) used improvisational dance as a means of analyzing and re-presenting the findings. Data were gathered from a community walk in which school teachers were asked to consider their students' communities, as a means of addressing the perceived cultural and linguistic gap between these teachers and their students. The teachers created a poster using their reflective notes and artefacts collected from the walk, which they presented to the wider teacher group. They were then asked to complete an open-ended survey which sought new insights gained from the walk. During the following summer, the same teachers were asked to repeat the exercise in the same communities to re-analyze their understanding of their school community. On completion of the second survey, the teachers were provided with their previous responses to compare findings. Using her own voice, Cancienne recorded 72 different teacher responses to three questions from the questionnaire. Having copied these to CD and with the aid of a digital camera, Cancienne used these two tools, along with her own experience as a dancer, to engage in an improvisational dance inspired by the teachers' words. The re-presentation was a means of embodying the participants' experiences and making sense of the data, enabling new themes to enlarge on previous understandings. Further, Cancienne sought to connect with the teachers' perspectives in an 'empathic, emotional way' (2008:177), and provided an opportunity to express the voice of the 'outlier cases' which had struck the researcher as 'evocatively important'. Using dance to interpret and represent the data provided an opportunity for Cancienne, a trained choreographer, dancer and researcher, to discover and present new meanings, through her use of performance, to both the research participants, as well as new and more diverse audiences.

> Barone and Eisner (2012) suggest that representation in arts-related research is therefore expressing what has been learnt through artistic ways which might otherwise be beyond words. The use of the arts *is* the purposeful act which seeks to engage the viewer to think (again), to take notice, to see afresh, to disrupt; to persuade the viewer to revisit the world from a different direction.

What is important in representation is thinking about 'aesthetic utility' (Barone & Eisner, 2012: 20) and how the art form can act as a mode of transportation (Ettinger, 2011). For example, the use of colloquial language in a piece of poetry may be used as a literary device which takes liberties with the reader and serves to 'transport' them to reassess the work. The researcher may use different lenses through which the viewer can learn differently about the issue being explored, for example using portraiture in a piece of visual art, or taking on the role of a 'witness' in a play. It may be that metaphor is used as a tool, which allows for the displacement of subject and object relations. Metaphor enables movement and awareness to shift and be re-examined; to make relationships accessible to our senses (Barrett, 2008). Similarly, emotions may be expressed rendered through poetic language or crescendo and diminuendo in a piece of music. In all these examples such renderings are carefully selected and serve important heuristic purposes. These devices, or tropes, are used to expand and to emphasise, to aid insight, to create disruption, to be playful.

Issues of quality also link to aesthetic considerations and the artist's involvement in the creation of the piece. Barone and Esiner (2012:145) argue that to be useful, arts-related research needs to 'succeed as a work of art and as a work of research'. In contrast, Carroll (2001) proposes that the use of imperfections in the artistic work can cause different raw and uncompromising responses to the phenomena. What is important is how the researcher labels the research as arts related. With this the artist needs to be mindful of quality criteria in representation. Putting ones work 'out there' is about being open to criticism and as English and Stengel (2010) contend, is healthy for art practice and no different from scholarly criticism present in any other discipline.

Beyond asserting its profile within scholarly realms, arts-related research provides important opportunities for the research to be shared within the public domain. With a broad audience reach, important issues of social and cultural significance can be shared. The challenge in representation in public venues is in not oversimplifying complex issues, and in finding ways to be challenging whilst not being off-putting. Finally, there are degrees of transparency which are more challenging to capture during this phase, hence we suggest it is important for the inquiry presentation to additionally capture the process of interpretation and expression of what has been learnt.

Mapping out the associative relations 'above and beyond' qualitative analysis processes exemplifies different and diverse ways of undertaking analysis, interpretation and representation in arts-related research. As a final example, Harrison provides his own story from his practice which illustrates this:

---

*Author Reflection*
**Spencer J. Harrison**, Faculty of Art, in Drawing and Painting at OCAD University, Toronto, Canada

As I turned the car from the well travelled dirt road onto the farm lane I looked in the rear-view mirror and watched the dust curl up around the back of the car. I remember how my sister and I would watch out the back window of the old Buick for that dust storm signalling we were almost there. As soon as the car stopped we would push open the doors, and I would race to my Grandfather in the fields or barn and she bounded to Grandma's side somewhere in the kitchen or out in the garden. This time would be different, as my almost eighty year old mother and I would politely exit the car and reintroduce ourselves to those who presently rented the farm and had generously agreed to let us walk the property. Mum and I would here share stories as one of the ways of conducting the research for my doctorate.

Through an autoethnographic (Chang, 2008), arts-informed (Cole & Knowles, 2008), dissertation, my research explores notions of growing up gay in rural Ontario, without the lens of an outsider's scrutiny of this experience, but rather with an insider view, looking back through a lens of time. This research contrasts some of the very negative ways I was imagined as a young gay man, with the more positive impressions I had of my life and myself at that time. The research has been completed through the painting of a Freak Show tent. On the outside of the tent I painted images appropriated from historical Ringling Brothers and Barnum and Bailey Circus advertisements, intertwined with three images of myself reflecting negative ways I am imagined as a gay man and echoing my nick name as a youth, "Freak Show." The inside is painted with images and narratives of my life from my earliest memories, to my teenage memories, when aged about fifteen, I first met another gay person and realised that I was not the only one. It is the retelling of the positive and resilient ways I navigated my world. The viewer or reader of my research traverses the interior and exterior of the tent exploring the contradictions in perception and the conundrums I had navigating these multiple identities. Although the use of these methodologies is not necessarily all that new in Europe, the United Kingdom, or the United States; in Canada, in the Faculty of Education, at the University of Toronto, they seemed rather controversial.

Suffice to say that, when the media started paying attention to the Freak Show tent I was painting as the main form of data collection, analysis, and dissemination

---

*Continued*

of my research findings, the university created extra hurdles of scrutiny of my dissertation.

This practice was clearly inequitable to the procedures of other doctoral candidates and I would posit unethical. My supervisor attempted to block this from happening citing the inability of the Dean of Research and Graduate Studies to have the expertise to scrutinize my research. As a way of compromise so the examination could take place, I asked the chair of my department to review my dissertation. In a superficial way he did so, assuring the Dean that my dissertation met the requirements of a doctorate. He never saw or was inside the tent.

After greeting one of the people who is renting the farm, my mum and I walked where the barn had been, now visible only by the old foundation; walked the perimeter of where the one acre garden had once stood, which was now just the beginning of a field; and walked out to the road and back. We told each other stories of our differing childhood memories on that land. We talked about whether we thought her parents, my grandparents, had any knowledge of my gay identity. And when we were about to get back into the car, we were asked if we wanted to come into the house and look there as well. Mum wasn't sure if she should say yes, though she was bursting to get a peek. Inside the house more stories were told, now with an audience close at hand. When she entered her childhood bedroom, the tears (she would be embarrassed to let strangers see) were unstoppable. She brushed them aside saying she never imagined she would ever be back in that room. Outside and back in the car heading down the dusty lane she told me she thought that part of her identity was over and would never be known. She then expressed her surprise that it could factor into my research. Pulling out onto the road the dust curled behind the car, cutting off the view and again closing off the memories we had shared.

As an established professional artist, an arts-informed project seemed only natural. As someone who has consistently painted about my life experiences, autoethnography did not seem like much of a stretch. This research project asked me to pull together my familiar ways of creating new knowledge with a strong contextualization of what I was producing. This project allowed me to explore deeper meaning making than would be available through more traditionally accepted means of research, since I could work with details no other researcher could attain. The dissemination of my findings through a painted project created opportunities for the research to be explored by a much broader audience. The healing nature of the work for myself, for my community, and for the greater population was far reaching. Through this strong arts-informed research work I bettered the human condition by sharing the narratives of my life and creating a site where its audience can tell their own stories.

CONCLUSION

This chapter has explored the analytical, interpretive and representational processes which occur when examining data as part of arts-related research. We have considered how analytical processes within arts-related research go above and beyond processes applied to qualitative analysis, by presenting a model of rendering, portrayal and praxis. Whilst time consuming as well as labour intensive, the sharing of research findings made accessible through use of art forms and practices with others can be powerful in broadening and deepening conversations. Such forms of representation provide possibilities for re-examining and extending meanings of research inquiry, providing different, competing and complementary modes of expression, interpretation, creative thought and action.

# ETHICS IN ARTS-RELATED RESEARCH

## INTRODUCTION

This chapter examines a range of concerns related to ethics in arts-related research. It begins by outlining some of the issues that are particular to this field and then examines the ways in which ethical and quality issues from other subjects and disciplines might be helpful in addressing concerns raised by the arts-based communities. Whilst we acknowledge that we draw on the education, social sciences and health domain in this area we also recognise that there are many researchers in arts-related research who struggle to delineatine ways in which ethics and quality might be approached. This this chapter aims to tackle some of these concerns and suggest possible ways forward.

## GENERAL ETHICAL ISSUES

There is a tendency in arts-related research to import and insert ethical concepts and principles from other disciplines, for example, from medicine and health in particular, who have been highly influential in research ethics. As a result using principles from more bounded disciplines can result in an unhelpful performativity about dealing with ethics, ethics board and issues of quality in arts-related research. Macfarlane for example, suggests that:

> Demonstrating that you have 'covered' research ethics in the language of biomedical science is now a de facto requirement for anyone seeking to pass a masters or doctoral thesis or get a paper published in a peer reviewed journal. This is about inauthentic, scripted communication. While the fast-food worker may be required to tell the customer to 'have a nice day!' academic researchers are required to state that they 'kept all data confidential' or that 'the identity of research subjects was anonymised'. Clichéd statements of this type represent little more than sham compliance with the audit of RECs, journal editors and reviewers, and lecturers who assess theses and dissertations. They demonstrate that the researcher understands the strategic 'game' and has chosen the politically correct language to convey the right impression to the reader (Lea, 2009). It is about a demonstration of emotional performativity. Researchers have shown that they 'care' about the impact of their research on others, whether they genuinely do so or not. (Macfarlane, 2010: 22)

Barone and Eisner (2012) suggest that arts-related research must succeed both as a work of art and as a work of research. This arguably requires the aesthetic work to be of sufficient standing to attract the audience to the phenomena portrayed and be robust enough to meet methodological scrutiny. Finley (2005:693) similarly raises a number of questions about what counts as good arts-related research and what artistic skill is required by those not educated in the art-form chosen. However, whilst the assessment of creative art works might be judged in relation to a range of criteria addressing rigour and art-criticism, careful attention to the ethics of the inquiry process are also warranted, especially when considering how the research might be judged a success from the perspective of the researcher, the researched and the audience (Sinding et al., 2008).

Whilst we suggest that there are ethical concepts that can be transferred from other disciplines there are particular concerns specific to arts-related research. For example in medicine there is often a belief that either something is ethical or it is not, but as Sierz suggests in relation to his examination of the play 'Blasted'

> ... the ethical problem is that *Blasted* can surely be read as both a denunciation of the horrors of war and a domestication of them. *Blasted* is not an example of brutalism, nor does it brutalize the audience, but – perhaps, and ironically – its effect in the culture might have been to help habituate us to extreme violence. And this habituation in culture might aid power to prepare us for even greater brutality in the real world. War becomes more acceptable, because more familiar. Our hunger to know more about extreme human behaviour might lead not to outrage, but to satiation. The ethical question would then be: is it enough to characterize any play as either/or good/bad? Surely, the complexity of theatre, and of audience reaction, is such that our habitually bipolar 'either/or' thinking should be replaced by a 'both/and' point of view? (Sierz, 2010: 112)

We suggest here a number of more traditional options for consideration, followed by some other options that may provide a better fit with arts related research.

## THE CHALLENGE OF ADOPTING 'TRADITIONAL ETHICS

Many of the current stances toward ethics are based in the philosophy of positivism, where the view is that something is only meaningful if it may be seen or measured (logical positivism) or that science should be focused on objectively determined observable phenomena and on measuring what one may observe (Comtean positivism) Thus positivists value objectivity, rationality, neutrality and 'truth' and seek to reduce knowledge to abstract and universal principles. A shift away from this was made by researchers calling themselves post-postivists who argued instead for a move away from objectivity. Yet in many ways post-positivism is simply a reaction to positivism; it is 'post' (after) positivism, and it is problematic because these researchers retain positivist stances such as the view that reality exists and may be discovered through logical processes. For example, Guba and

Lincoln (1994; 2005) have suggested that while post-positivists typically use modified experimental designs aimed at falsification of hypotheses, they may also use qualitative methods. It is these researchers who drew on positivism and argued for a different stance for qualitative research and whose work the terms below generally relate to:

*Reliability and Validity*

Reliability and Validity are both terms from the positivist paradigm. Reliability ensures the experiments can be repeated to measure the same thing again accurately: measurements should be consistent and repeatable; in other words, an instrument should measure the same thing each time it is used with the same subjects in similar conditions. Validity is the term used to describe the development of criteria for judging the soundness of qualitative research. Validity determines whether the research truly measures what it was intended to measure or how truthful the research results are. Strategies are developed to ensure there is some kind of qualifying check to ensure the research is sound and credible, so that the researcher can argue for the strength of the findings. The challenge in adopting the concept of validity to qualitative research in general and arts-related research in particular is that by definition it deals with truth claims. For research to be valid or validated, it must be grounded in 'truth'; thus it relies upon a 'Trust me, I am a good researcher' mentality (Major and Savin-Baden, 2010a:74). So while the term 'validity' has some value for qualitative research and while it has been applied in the field of inquiry, the concept increasingly has been replaced by the term 'trustworthiness' (Lincoln & Guba, 1985) and more recently by terms such as plausibility (Savin-Baden & Major, 2013).

*Trustworthiness*

The notion of trustworthiness suggests that the researcher must make an effort to gain trust, rather than to establish 'truth'. The basic question for documenting trustworthiness, according to Lincoln and Guba, is simply this: 'How can an inquirer persuade his or her audiences that the research findings of an inquiry are worth paying attention to?' (Lincoln & Guba, 1985, p. 290). Lincoln and Guba (1985) recommended four approaches for accomplishing trustworthiness: credibility, transferability, dependability, and confirmability. These concepts have stood the test of time and are still in use more than 30 years after their development, documenting that qualitative researchers believe it important to document quality of qualitative research. However we suggest that trustworthiness is still problematic as it is still based on ideas that fit a post-positivist perspective, which holds with the position that we cannot separate ourselves from what we know in our search for objectivity.

## Bias and Rigour

These are concepts that are used to suggest that if researchers are sufficiently diligent, then they will be able to uncover some version of the truth and that they will try not to be biased. This stance positions the researcher as someone who is almost outside the situation looking in, rather than acknowledging that the researcher, whether interviewer, observer, artist, performer is part of the research process. What is important is that rigour extends to issues of ownership, integrity, transparency, plausibility and honesties as we discuss below and that what is sought is not a position of some kind of utopian objective bias, but of the ideal of gaining a better set of biases.

## Beneficence and Non-maleficence

The principles of beneficence and non-maleficence are closely related; beneficence involving balancing the benefits of engagement with any risks and costs involved, whereas non-maleficence means avoiding the causation of harm. Respecting the principles of beneficence and non-maleficence may in certain circumstances mean failing to respect a person's autonomy, anonymity and decision to take part. People may initially feel overwhelmed or baffled by what is taking place. Certainly being involved in a project might at times be unpleasant, uncomfortable or even painful for those involved, but similarly involvement might create opportunity for personal growth and renewal which would not occur otherwise.

## Veracity

Veracity addresses attributes such as integrity, trustworthiness and loyalty and in relation to arts-related research can be considered in relation to the way in which the artful representations and research findings represent what has been experienced, and by whom. It is important that the art-researched work can account for participants' decisions over what is to be presented and made public. There is a responsibility of the artist/researcher and the research participants to take a stand, but not to overstate what has occurred, nor to avoid exaggerating power differentials, for example in terms of how an audience is expected to 'witness' the work (Park-Fuller, 2000).

## Participant Validation and Member Checking

These two terms are often confused and used interchangeably. The basic premise is that researchers need to check the trustworthiness of data with participants. Participant validation involves returning data, such as interview transcripts to participants to check it represents what they said accurately. Member checking moves beyond mere verification and seeks affirmation of the ways data are interpreted and presented. This implies by doing this that the research is thought to be more credible. Whilst this approach allows participants a voice in what the findings say and the opportunity to correct any possible mis-interpretations on the part of the researcher, it also could be said to be patronising, since it assumes that research participants are in some way vulnerable. It is therefore a delicate balance and the researcher has to ask how much of their own interpretations are they prepared to have changed or deleted by a participant – especially if they believe some dishonesty has been going on

## Triangulation

This is a mathematical term, used in surveying and adopted by researchers. The idea is that a point can be located from the angles subtended from *three* known points, but measured at the new unknown point rather than the previously fixed points. In research the idea is then that by gaining data from a number of different perspectives (such as 3) it will necessarily be more accurate, valid and reliable. Denzin (1978) identified 4 types of triangulation:

1. Data triangulation - using a variety of people, status, different points of view
2. Investigator triangulation - using several researchers
3. Theory triangulation - using different perspectives to interpret the data
4. Methodological triangulation - using multiple methods and approaches

The underlying belief here is that by having multiple data points the researcher will have more credible understanding of the subject of their research. However, triangulation tends to encourage the cleaning up of data, tidying data into themes and ignoring those data which do not fit. There is an assumption that data, people, contexts and methods can be triangulated and that taking up such an approach will necessarily result in some kind of validity yet in arts-related research the work, the context and participants tend to overlap and merge, thus assumptions about the possibility for adopting triangulation are misplaced.

## Informed Consent

There is often an assumption made by researchers, once consent has been gained and a form signed, that this consent is both informed and lasts for the duration of the project. The question is whether individuals ever fully consent. We suggest that consent can never be something that is fully informed, as participants rarely completely understand what they have signed up for or indeed what is published as a result of what they have said, even if they have signed a form stating that they do. What is important, we believe, is that the ethical stance of a researcher centres on social responsibility and a recognition that consent varies across cultures and context. For example, asking for consent from the village chief will be vital for research in areas such as the Easter Cape in South Africa and realising that consent will be implied in context where community members are unable to write. Macfarlane (2010: 20) also suggests that asking participants to sign a consent form is 'a defensive and quasi-legal means of trying to 'protect' the university, and to some extent the researcher, from litigation or other accusations of wrong-doing'.

Thus it is evident that many of these ways of ensuring sound ethical procedures observed in qualitative research still lean toward post-positivism - which is a somewhat bounded position and one which many who work in the qualitative paradigm reject. Whilst it is important to be aware of these concepts, we suggest that arts-related research is more readily located in social constructionism and constructivism and thus different ways of seeing, doing and managing ethics are required which we present below.

## PARTICULAR ETHICAL CONCERNS WHEN UNDERTAKING ARTS-BASED RESEARCH

Ethical issues need to be considered throughout the project lifetime and should not be seen as a necessary precursory step related to initial project approval. In addition, adherence to sound ethics is not just about facilitating the research process with the researched, but rather placing equal importance on providing a 'protective' function for the researcher (Cousin, 2009).

The notion of whether truth exists and whether it can be ascertained is one that has been discussed and debated ad nauseum. While the concepts such as triangulation and validity are value laden and may be seen as undesirable and unachievable it is still clear that researchers undertaking arts-related research do need some guiding principles in the realm of ethics. We suggest the following areas need to be considered:

– Ownership
– Reflexivity
– Negotiated meaning
– Transparency
– Plausibility
– Honesties
– Integrity
– Verisimilitude
– Criticality
– Stance
– Authenticity
– Peer evaluation

### Ownership

Whether as an artist, artist-research or researcher who becomes part of the work it is important to consider who owns not only the work but also the data in conventional research, data is generally collected from or with the participants, yet in arts-related research, researchers and participants may be performers or artists and therefore data is part of the process, product and often their own personal journey. It is important at the outset of any project to decide how data will be collected, who owns them, how they will be shared, presented, disseminated and re-used. Such issues and concerns may make us uncomfortable but they also introduce questions that need to be considered, and thus some further questions worthy of exploration might include:

— What strategies have been taken to ensure that all those involved are located within the research?
— What steps, and by whom, have been taken to ensure that participants, the work and the voices are portrayed honestly?
— In what ways have people's contributions and stories been located in the research findings and dissemination?

---

*Example*

In 2013 Katherine and I (Maggi) attended a conference and participated in a workshop entitled *Methodologies That Move: Circus and Celebration of Unthinkable Qualitative Inquiry.* The session was described as follows:

*This session is staged as a circus of methodologies that move. With methodologies conceptualized as in flux researchers face interesting openings and stimulating puzzlements. Four qualitative researchers present their work in the form of performances, stunts, and/or other circus formats and a ringmaster draws in audience participants. The subject matter includes (1) unthinkable 'data analysis' resulting from doctoral students' unpredictable interactions with data, (2) audience participation in making a material artifact of 'truth-telling' and risk in qualitative research, (3) a freak show of affect in a series of encounters with narrative portraits and visual images of people who use heroin (and other opiates), and (4) a geek performance that theorizes the role of 'citation' in critical qualitative inquiry.*

*Aaron Kuntz explained his part of the sessions as follows:*

*In this presentation I ask participants to co-create a working collage regarding the material realities of risk and truth-telling. I begin with an overview of my paper. I then invite the audience to create artistic renditions of truth-telling in their own work, using provided materials. Individually, collages represent participants' own inquiry projects and practices. Collectively, collages display a larger movement of truth-telling and relational risk-taking via inquiry. . .*

*Continued*

It was a challenging and innovative session, which disrupted our thinking and helped to consider and reconsider our stances and views. It was a highly interactive session and what we shared became part of the process and the presentation. There was no sense that the authors who ran the session sought out consent to take our views away and use and portray them. However, we suspect the ideas and views shared did ultimately add to the final papers they published somewhere in some journal. Whilst we were happy to be part of this process it did introduce a number of questions about ownership, portrayal, sharing and ownership when participating in such a seminar without any recourse to perhaps some of our left behind ideas and intellectual property ...

*Reflexivity*

Reflexivity is the process by which we as researchers seek to challenge, continually, our biases and examine our stances, perspectives, and views as a researcher. Reflexivity as a concept suggests that the position or perspective of the researcher shapes everything; as Nightingale and Cromby (1999: 228) suggest reflexivity:

> requires an awareness of the researcher's contribution to the construction of meanings throughout the research process, and an acknowledgment of the impossibility of remaining 'outside of' one's subject matter while conducting research. Reflexivity then, urges us 'to explore the ways in which a researcher's involvement with a particular study influences, acts upon and informs such research'.

Reflexivity refers both to the researchers awareness of their relationship to the field of study and those with whom they research, as well as their awareness of themselves and the impact of their cultural practices within the research setting. Although reflexivity is an approach to ensuring ethical behaviour and quality in qualitative research, and has been an ideal that was first suggested in the natural sciences and was adopted and developed in anthropology, we still believe it has particular relevance in arts-related research, because of the ways in which the artistic process and the research process overlap one another.

*Negotiated Meaning*

When we, as researchers, write and create accounts of the settings and people who are part of the research there is a need to negotiate meaning. Part of the process of interpretation demands that as we begin to make sense of the language, image, or visualisation used by participants and engage with the subtext, we begin to see the gaps in our interpretation and the flaws in what we are seeking to present. It is often the case that our accounts do not coincide with the perspectives of our participants.

For some researchers it seems acceptable to censor their own interpretations if participants do not agree with them. For other researchers reaching some kind of agreement is seen as a vital part of the reflexive process. Yet the options about how interpretations are managed are complex and multifaceted so that decisions about power over, and ownership of, data and (interpretation thereof) tends to relate to the nature of the research topic, the type of data as well as those involved. It is through negotiation of what would count as a more honest account that we begin to make the shift away from description and analysis towards an interpretative account. Yet with some topics the nature of honesties and truths may remain contested ground. It is only by realising that both researcher and participant perspectives are complex and contested that we can come to know our own shifting stances and realize that our beliefs and values are relative. Thus, for us, shared truths are achieved most often through dialogue.

*Transparency*

We believe that it is critical to be transparent, what Savin-Baden and Fisher (2002) and Major and Savin-Baden (2010a, 2010b) call 'honesties' in research There are a number of ways that transparency can be achieved in the research process (Savin-Baden & Fisher 2002; Major & Savin-Baden 2010a; 2010b). For example, we can situate ourselves in relation to participants. Doing so requires an awareness of power relationships during interviews; the unique context of the researcher and the researched, and should lead to the researcher striving for a clear view of what participants mean while simultaneously seeking and acknowledging co-created meaning. We also may engage in self-disclosure, which involves the researcher in disclosing their positionality with participants as well as voicing mistakes. To be transparent, we also need to situate ourselves in relation to the data, which calls for a consideration of data ownership and how they are to be used. This requires taking a critical stance towards research, acknowledging our philosophical stance and our efforts toward criticality.

*Plausibility*

Plausibility emphasises the idea of ensuring quality across the research, from the beginning to the end and acknowledging that the knower and the known are interlinked and truth(s) is/are negotiated through dialogue. Plausibility (Major & Savin-Baden, 2010b) is the process of ensuring your research is rigorous and robust so that you can manage the research honestly. In the past qualitative research has used 'validity' but it is a term that has too much resonance with the quantitative paradigm and tends to ignore the complexities of qualitative research. However, issues connected with plausibility also collide with ethical concerns. For example, not only is it important to examine issues about ownership in arts-related research it is also vital to understand the ways in which data have been managed and interpreted.

It is common in articles that are publishing research to present findings through photographs, artwork, excerpts from a play or an unmediated interview transcript. Whilst this can be a useful means of representation, what is invariably omitted is any kind of interpretation. This lack of interpretation, in ethical terms, brings into question the plausibility of the research itself. In arts-related research it cannot be assumed that 'the data speaks for itself'; it does not. Thus in order for research to be plausible, rigorous and credible, interpretation must be provided.

*Honesties*

Honesties (following Stronach et al. 2002) as a concept requires researchers to acknowledge not only the cyclical nature of 'truths' but also that the nature of honesties is defined by people and contexts and helps us to avoid the prejudice *for* similarity and *against* difference in data interpretation. Furthermore, data about ethics, conduct and accountability can be distinguished by differences of theory and practical action, but they can never actually be isolated from one another. Issues such as these in both research and practice demand that we engage with deceptions – our own and those involved in the research – and this in turn forces us to consider how we deal with such (benevolent) deception.

*Integrity*

Researcher integrity is a concept that identifies the researcher as a person who will necessarily enable a unique interpretation of a data set (Johnson 1999; Whittemore et al. 2001). Therefore the researcher must strive for integrity, which may be accomplished, for example, by ensuring that interpretations are grounded within the data and reflected in the text. Maintaining integrity is a complex activity, partly because our perspectives change and move as we undertake the research and partly because the research and the researched change and move as well. This kind of interpretation involves situating ourselves not just in the stages of the research, but also in relation to the data we analyzed and interpreted during and after data collection. This may sound obvious, but too often we ignore our own stances and perspectives and act as if we are sitting outside the data (and not acknowledging that we are interpreting and judging as we read). It is often easier to adopt complicated coding strategies than to engage with the messiness and complexity of reinterpreting data. Analyzing them in a simplistic way just leaves lists of themes, thin description and little, if any broader cultural interpretation.

*Verisimilitude*

Verisimilitude, although an unwieldy term, simply argues for seeking truths, or the quality of seeming to be true, by examining more and more truths for the purpose of excluding those that ultimately prove not to be truthful. In this way, the researcher then comes closer to discovering plausible truths. The concept of verisimilitude thus can be used as a vehicle through which an analysis framework may be scrutinised and findings examined in more depth. Denzin, in fact, proposed deconstructive verisimilitude as a strategy that might be used to provide legitimate answers to the research questions. This strategy is accomplished through interrogation of that which 'seems to be true', considering conditions under which it might not be true or that which 'seems not to be true' that might indeed be true. He uses the analogy of a murder mystery novel to illustrate the use of verisimilitude as a standard of truth. He explained that what seems to be true in such novels is usually shown to be untrue, while what seems untrue is often found to be true. However, we suggest that arts-related research needs to be seen as a means of uncovering a range of views, rather than seeking to negotiate what counts as truth. Thus whilst verisimilitude is helpful to a degree we argue that criticality is a more useful ethical stance in arts-related research.

*Criticality*

Criticality is related to verisimilitude and is the idea that researchers should strive for critical analysis and awareness while conducting and reviewing research. The word 'critical' itself derives directly from a set of Greek words including *Krisis* a turning-point, *Kritikos* a judge or decision-maker, and *Krinein* to discriminate. In conceptions of criticality too, scholars have indicated the need to position findings in ways that negotiations are sought, rather than seen as affirmation of truth. In discussing criticality, Barnett (1997) has argued for three levels of criticality, as follows:

*Critical thinking* — These are cognitive acts undertaken by the individual. We suggest that researchers engaged in critical thinking may do so in the company of other researchers and artists and their critical thinking may be enhanced through that interchange; but the emphasis in the term critical thinking is on the character of the individual's cognitive acts.

*Critical thought* — This has a wider focus than just the individual's thought processes. Critical thought is collaborative and takes place within the discipline of study. For example, individuals might be doing some hard critical thinking but critical thought develops and takes off through sustained interchange around collective perspectives. Critical thought necessarily contains a social component and thus can only be developed collaboratively.

*Critique* — Critique is a form of criticism about the discipline, or the research itself, seeking to set it in a wider context rather than merely having internal debates within the discipline. In critique, different views of an issue or situation may be proffered as alternative perspectives are taken on board. This is a cognitive and personal challenge, and it may open up the way to a transformation of the individual student. We suggest in arts-related research it is this level of criticality that should be sought. Researchers need to be able to critique their discipline, position and stance and be prepared to be challenged through both the research process and the artistic process. Engaging with critique can often seem risky, but we suggest it is central to the kind of arts-related research that seeks to be transformative. Thus within this idea of criticality it is important to recognise shifts along the trajectory from transition to transformation:

– Transitional critique is when a challenge or query prompts us to reconsider views and perspectives and there is movement from one position to another. The concept of transition carries with it the idea of movement from one place to another, and with it the necessity of taking up a new position in a different place. Leaving an existing position and entering the transitions can be troublesome but is where personal change takes place.
– Transformational critique is more complex and involves an identity shift. This happens when challenges occur to value and belief systems. Identity shifts are characterised by not only a change in perception of self and others, but also changes in perspectives about the political, social and economic ways in which life is lived. Transformational critique is often caused by a moral dilemma thus a major challenge to one's position and identity occurs, often resulting in a sense of confusion and a need to rethink one's stance radically.

*Stance*

The position, stance and influence of the researcher also have received considered attention in social science research. The stance of the researcher is about how we position ourselves in relation to the methodology, participants and methods. It also relates to how we manage and construct data analysis and interpretation. Researcher stance is important as it helps us to see not only the (relative) plausibility, but also to see whether there is honesty and consistency between methods and researcher. However, in arts-related research stance is also bound up with the artistic process and the ways in which we position our self in relation to this. The issue of stance introduces questions about whether ethically there is a need to be an artist in order to undertake arts-related research, whether one must work with an artist if one is not an artist or whether anyone can undertake arts-rated research as long as they understand the artistic process and their position as researcher in relation to it. Stance reflects people's core values, which are derived from a range of personal characteristics (such as culture, upbringing, political views, occupation, race and gender).

*Authenticity*

This is the notion that research should reflect the lived experiences of the participants. The researcher should exhibit an awareness of the difference in voices of participants, no matter how subtle. The notion is that multiple realities must be portrayed and researchers need to explore how people's perspectives of themselves and others shape the contexts in which they live. Research often comprises contradictory stories so that researchers and participants seem 'caught between stories, split between grounding narrative that offer(ed) different versions of a professional self along with tangential manifestations of a personal self' (Stronach et al, 2001: 16). However, often in ethnodrama and ethno theatre this can be troublesome. White and Belliveau (2010) examined issues which we suggest relate to the concept of authenticity in a project that used theatre to fictionalize the 'inner voices' of educators. The underlying idea was to reveal diverse perspectives and loyalties in educational settings and to do this the researchers designed a scene (The Principal's Office) to serve as a site of inquiry to explore inner voices. The authors examined the issue of fictionalizing voices but through the process realised that the artistic process and the research process raised ethical concerns at the same time, relating to the issues of authenticity. The authors explain it as follows:

> The inner voices in 'The Principal's Office' primarily represent that which is left unsaid in a dialogue because the thinker deems it inappropriate or potentially damaging to the professional relationship. However, the whole process of negotiating the tensions around taking a new investigative approach heightened the author's awareness of another form of inner voice, one that plays a productive role in fostering reflexivity and compromise. In this situation, the author found himself compelled by the inner voice to contemplate certain questions that in the end featured significantly in helping to resolve some of the interpersonal tensions that had emerged. The inner voice proved instrumental in highlighting the inconsistency of laying claim to what had previously been presented as a universal story (White & Belliveau, 2010: 93)

Thus exploring issues of authenticity in arts-related research prompts researchers to examine what it is they are laying claim to and enables them to examine issues of power and the subtext of the research and artistic process in relation to one another. It prompts researcher and artist to examine what counts as authenticity, and for whom.

## Peer Evaluation

An additional step toward ensuring credibility can involve using peers in several phases of the process. Experts, colleagues, participants and other artists should examine the findings, the interpretation and the ways the findings are presented. Attention should also be given to what was not said, presented or performed, as well as what was. Peer evaluation helps researchers to consider questions such as:

- What truths have been expressed with little scrutiny?
- Which findings seem improbable?
- What subtext has been ignored
- What has not been analysed
- What contradictions are revealed? Under what conditions might these be reconciled?
- What has not been presented?

Considering all these issues will ensure that those using arts-related research will be able to engage with the diverse range of issues involved in ethics in this area. The ability to argue for this kind of research can be problematic in some settings but using these and considering the challenges raised in Table 6.1 below can help researchers and artists deal with the queries often raised by ethics boards and committees.

*Table 6.1. Ethics concepts and challenges in arts-related research*

| Ethical issue | Definition | Challenge for arts-related researchers |
|---|---|---|
| Ownership | The ethical agreement about who has rights over research data. | The consideration of who owns data and how they will be shared, presented, disseminated and re-used. |
| Reflexivity | The means by which researchers challenge biases, stances and perspectives in the research process. | The extent to which they are able to be honest about how reflexive they are and their ability to examine their shortcomings as a reflexive researcher. |
| Negotiated meaning | The process of sharing, discussing and negotiating research findings. | The ability to hear and respond to participants' feedback realistically, and with honesty |
| Transparency | Striving for a clear view of what participants mean while simultaneously acknowledging co-created meaning. | The ability to engage in self-disclosure, which involves the researcher in disclosing their positionality with participants as well as voicing mistakes. |
| Plausibility | Recognising that the knower and the known are interlinked and truth is negotiated through dialogue. | Negotiating the ways data are managed and interpreted across power relationships and competing agendas. |
| Honesties | Acknowledgement by researchers of the cyclical nature of 'truths' and the impact of people and contexts on truths. | The need to be aware of the possibilities of deception in research – our own as well as those we work with. |
| Integrity | Analysing data in an interpretive way that does justice to the participants and their contexts. | Ensuring that easy computer analysis programmes or simplistic analysis strategies are not adopted over the complexity of in-depth data interpretation. |

*(Continued)*

*Table 6.1. (Continued)*

| Ethical issue | Definition | Challenge for arts-related researchers |
|---|---|---|
| Verisimilitude | The ability to acknowledge and seek truths through interrogation. | Ignoring issues which seem not to be true rather than seeking to interrogate data, stances, positions and plausibility of people and contexts. |
| Criticality | The ability to take a critical stance towards one's own position, acknowledge biases and recognise that alternative perspectives may need to be taken on board. | Ignoring criticism and criticality at the expense of gaining new perspectives and a better set of biases. |
| Stance | The way the researcher positions themselves in relation to the methodology, participants and methods. It also relates to how we manage and construct data analysis and interpretation. | The temptation to ignore stance and philosophical position and instead just to adopt methods that are not methodology related or appropriate. |
| Authenticity | This is the notion that research should reflect experiences of the participants. The researcher should exhibit an awareness of the difference in voices of participants, no matter how subtle. | The tendency to ignore contradiction and difference in order to ensure the presentation of data seems smooth and coherent instead of contradictory. |
| Peer evaluation | The process of using peer and critical friends to critique the study in its entirety. | The temptation to ignore peer perception or if peer evaluation is used, to ignore the criticism. |

## CONCLUSION

This chapter has presented a range of ethical issues that need to be considered when undertaking arts-related research. Whilst it is invariably impossible to cover all of these, recognising the importance of them and attempting to engage with as many as possible is a useful starting point. To ignore ethical concerns in arts-related studies is foolhardy, but it is important for researchers and research teams to consider their ethical stance, which issues are important, and how such issues are to be managed. Most research ethics boards and committees will raise questions but it is important that those undertaking the research should have anticipated the answers to ethical dilemmas before such questions are posed.

# ARTS-RELATED RESEARCH IN DIFFERENT DISCIPLINES AND CONTEXTS

## INTRODUCTION

There are many textbooks that cover a range of arts-informed inquiry and explore its use in different disciplines. However, this chapter will draw on case study material from a number of international projects in order to show how arts-related research may be used effectively in diverse disciplines and complex contexts such as areas of poverty, disability, and political complexity. In particular it explores the areas of dance, youth work, health, medicine and law, and suggests ways in which some of these projects may inform future research in these areas by adopting a more transdisciplinary focus than earlier studies.

## DISCIPLINE-BASED PEDAGOGY AND ARTS-RELATED RESEARCH

Many of the issues about how arts-related approaches are used in different disciplines begin with exploring the philosophical position of that discipline at the outset. Discipline-based pedagogy is defined here as the way in which the discipline informs and guides teacher knowledge and beliefs, about what to do and how to do it, in their subject area. Discipline-based pedagogy is typically introduced as a part of an induction programme into the norms of a discipline, and affects writing conventions, language and practices (which are often covert). There has been increasing discussion about discipline-based pedagogy in the United Kingdom (UK), particularly in the debates about the relationship between research and teaching. Jenkins and Zetter (2003) argue that disciplines shape the nature of pedagogy and such pedagogies reflect the practices and culture of the discipline. Thus teacher knowledge and beliefs about what to do, how to do it and under which circumstances, can affect the way that students learn a particular subject matter. Shulman's works (1986; 1987) in the United States of America provide a framework for understanding teacher knowledge. In these he describes several layers of teacher knowledge that include both subject knowledge and pedagogical knowledge. Subject or content knowledge comprises the theories, principles and concepts of a particular discipline. In addition to this subject matter knowledge, general pedagogical knowledge or knowledge about teaching itself is another important aspect of teacher knowledge. While subject knowledge and pedagogical knowledge are perhaps self-evident, Shulman (1986: 6) asks: 'why this sharp distinction between content and pedagogical process?' Somewhere between subject matter knowledge and pedagogical knowledge sits discipline-based pedagogy, what Shulman termed 'pedagogical content knowledge,' which he describes as:

> the ways of representing and formulating the subject that make it comprehensible to others ... Pedagogical content knowledge also includes an understanding of what makes the learning of specific topics easy or difficult: the conceptions and preconceptions that students of different ages and backgrounds bring with them to the learning of those most frequently taught topics and lessons. (Shulman, 1986: 9-10)

Despite moves, in the UK at least, towards flexible pedagogies and the adoption of diverse types of research, considerable resistance does seem to remain. The focus seems to be on shoring up the disciplines and using outcomes, benchmarking and standards to pin down knowledge, research and quality, rather than open them up. This wish to operate on what seems to be a behavioural framework whilst expecting research creativity appears impossible. Such stances seem to emanate from a misplaced notion of 'the discipline'. While disciplines are seen to be vital, there appears to be little in-depth questioning of what a discipline is in the 21$^{st}$ Century. Disciplines comprise bodies of knowledge, traditions, values and discourses, yet these transcend and change and overlap with other disciplines and discourses. It is not clear whether (and which) disciplines need to be preserved and if they do, why this is the case. It seems questionable whether in studying physics or psychology the research has to be located in given and often covert disciplinary norms.

One of the areas where we see the breaking down of disciplinary boundaries and the merging of subject knowledge and pedagogical knowledge for both staff and students is in arts-related research. Thus, below we suggest a number of ways in which arts-related research might be presented, that transcend the need for the disciplines to be central and a guiding force.

## DISCIPLINARY EXAMPLES

There is a broad range of literature that suggests that artistic activities enhance the lives of older people in terms of health, quality of life and function, for example, through gardening, music and dance (Batt-Rawden and Tellnes, 2005; Greaves and Farbus, 2006; Kilroy et al., 2007; Daykin et al., 2008). Health gains have also been evident through the use of music and singing (Skingley and Vella-Burrows, 2010) and theatre performance has been used to stimulate discussion of problems depicted by older adults and their possible solutions (Palmar and Nascimento, 2002). In the UK, creative activities and health are an integral element of government policy and health guidelines (Department of Health Arts Council England, 2007; 2011 National Arts Policy Roundtable; National Institute for Health and Clinical Excellence [NICE], 2008; Social Exclusion Unit, 2004). Yet despite research interest in the value of arts for health, the field is relatively under-developed, not least due to the inherently complex and subtle nature of artistic and creative endeavours, which include:

– The huge range of art forms
– Individuality of different healthcare and community settings
– Diversity of individuals participating in projects
– The range of health issues that might be addressed (Clift et al., 2009:13)

*Health*

A range of studies indicate that there are many benefits for health in using the arts. For example, through the use of dance in patients with chronic heart failure (Belardinelli et al., 2008); and prompting social and psychological wellbeing for children with communication difficulties (Barnes, 2013). Art has been used to improve young people's wellbeing using a social capital approach (Hampshire and Matthijsse, 2010), with patients whilst on renal dialysis (Rowe et al., 2011) and with mental health services users (Stacey and Stickley, 2010). These studies demonstrate how arts projects have encouraged people to participate in ways that are creative, rewarding and inclusive. However, as noted in reviews conducted by Macnaughton et al. (2005) and Clift et al. (2009), few studies have identified directly measurable health gains which are required to convince policy makers of the need to support the arts and health sector effectively.

In recent years there has been growing interest in the contribution of the arts to the health of communities and individuals, as well as in the value of the arts in addressing significant social issues (Arts Council England, 2007; Clift 2006; Clift et al., 2006; Clift et al., 2009). Yet the evidence base for the effectiveness of particular interventions that target social isolation needs strengthening (Dickens et al., 2011), in particular when considering (measurable) means for elders to develop relationships that can enhance self-esteem, well-being and social inclusion (Sviden, Tham, and Borell, 2004). Thus there is a need to conduct robust studies that provide evidence of the importance for successful ageing and the maintenance of an active lifestyle physically, mentally and socially (Health Development Agency, 2004).

McNaughton et al. (2005) presented the arts and health diamond (Figure 7.1). The first dimension focuses on engagement with the arts and the second on individuals and either their personal well-being or their interaction with groups and communities.

An example of an arts and health project is the Creative Gymnasium project, delivered by the Belgrade Theatre, Coventry, UK. Their aim was to examine the benefits of drama and arts activities for improving and maintaining the physical and mental health and well-being of two of Coventry's priority health areas: teenage pregnancy and sexual health; and the 50+ age group. The Coventry University research team used arts-informed evaluation to examine participants' and stakeholders' perspectives. The findings from the study (Wimpenny and Savin-Baden, 2014) indicated that participants' engagement in an artistic occupation was self-validating. Further, theatre and performance provided opportunities for diverse marginalised members of a

# Key dimensions of arts/health

**Unity is health** – projects that start from the point of using creativity to enhance social relationships. These reflect a growing school of thought that good relationships are a major determinant on health.

**Creativity and well being** – projects that emphasise creativity as a route to well being. These aim to work with individuals to better understand their health, using creative approaches as a means to expression. Art is seen as a potential therapy.

**Engaging groups** – projects that engage groups to bring communities and health promotion closer together. They use creative methods to explore, disseminate, and communicate messages about health.

**Supporting care** – projects that support the process of care by working on the softer aspects of ill-health that health services, under the strain of heavy demand, cannot reach. Projects in the third group share some common ground, but aim to communicate with communities as a whole.

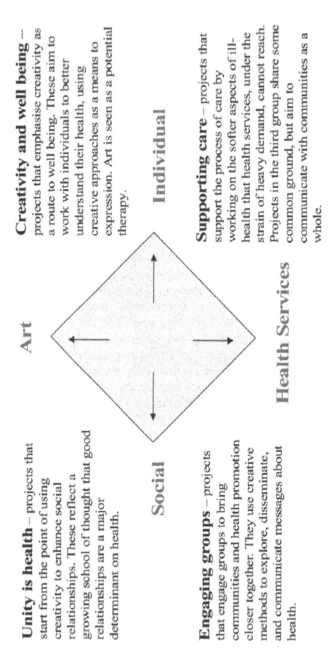

Art

Individual

Health Services

Social

*Figure 7.1. The arts and health diamond (McNaughton et al., 2005)*

community to connect and participate in a shared activity, thereby transforming their views of themselves and others. What is of note is the importance of space and place within this project, that is, the participants found a place to express themselves, to be themselves, to find out things about themselves and to feel respected members of their community. Moreover, the opportunity to produce and create credible public performance was also emphasised, with support from a professional artist as a workshop facilitator. The evidence and recommendations from the project, in combination with new partnerships established, has contributed to the Belgrade Theatre's decision to make an ongoing commitment to the delivery of arts activity to the 50+ population; this group being a key part of the delivery infrastructure for the city.

In a different example, Lorenzo (2010) used storytelling and creative activities as both data triggers and for data representation. Her study involved using participatory research with disabled women living in informal settlements in Cape Town, South Africa, concerning their experience of poverty and discrimination in relation to race, gender and disability. Lorenzo presents the interrelationship of arts-based media as both triggers for data collection and the data presentation; then further as a means of representation in Table 7.1 below.

*Table 7.1. Arts-related media for data collection and representation*

| DATA PRODUCTION | | | |
|---|---|---|---|
| Data generation | Data triggers | Facilitation techniques | Data capturing methods |
| Storytelling groups | Drawings | Small group discussions | Videotaping Audiotaping Scribing |
| Narrative action reflection workshops | Drawings Clay work Clay sculptures Singing Music Movement Drama Critical incident stories Writing songs Writing poems | Buzz groups Pairing Small group discussions (maximum of 8 people in a group) Plenary groups Brainstorming | Field notes Photographs |
| Reflective journal | | | |
| Data: transcripts of videotapes, audio files; fieldnotes and commentary on photographs | | | |
| Verification of data | | | |
| **Data analysis** | | **Data interpretation** | |
| Six step analysis of 'triggers' Thematic analysis Reflective stance approach | | Literature Consultative dialogues | |

101

In nursing, MacDonnell and Macdonald (2011) used guided imagery, images, narratives and poetry to explore people's insights into spiritual and ecological values, sexual orientation and culture. The authors used a variety of practical activities in order to challenge students' thinking and used Socratic methods to attempt to support the development of transformative learning. The authors describe a number of teaching approaches (use of dialogue, guided imagery and poetry) which could be adopted and adapted by others, but do not really explore the impact of this approach on learning and transformative change in people's lives.

The impact of conducting arts-related research across disciplinary borders both supports learning and transition for those involved as participants or as viewers, and also leads to self-reflective learning and critique of practices for the researcher(s) themselves. In the following author reflection, the creative impact which occurred when an artist researcher worked with a social science researcher to explore the impact of the arts on self and others is illustrated.

***Author Reflection***
Elelwani L. Ramugondo, University of Cape Town, South Africa

Person-as-artist informed inquiry was first coined in conversation with Katherine Wimpenny during her visit to the University of Cape Town in 2013. As she listened to me share critical lines of inquiry and methodologies in collaboration with a local performance poet and writer, Malika Ndovu, Katherine mentioned the work she and Maggi were involved in, delineating different forms of arts-based research. Katherine and I spent some time exploring possible points of convergence and divergence between person-as-artist informed inquiry and the taxonomy described (as presented in Chapter 1). On the 8th of August 2013, accompanied by Malika, I presented a public lecture as one of the Medical Humanities series hosted by the Gordon Institute for Performing and Creative Arts, http://www.gipca.uct.ac.za/project/medical-humanities-series-elelwani-ramugondo/ making the case for the potential contribution of the person-as-artist informed inquiry in exploring critical questions about health and healing.

Person-as-artist informed inquiry captures work Malika and I started during 2010, inspired and spurred on by both a deep curiosity about ways of being in the world for an artist, and to explore the impact of the arts on self and others. We saw great potential for the arts as a resource for self-healing work and perhaps even healing for communities and society in the context of prevalent structural and person-to-person violence, the extreme form of which is child rape in South Africa. I had also been in a number of spaces where art performance helped mourn a loss or shifted ways of seeing and experiencing the world in meaningful ways.

*Continued*

A real interest for Malika and I has been, and continues to be, on the human as a subject to the arts, inverting the dominant view where the arts are only seen as subservient. We have observed ourselves; especially I who otherwise may not be regarded an artist, being transformed profoundly once we surrendered to what is evoked in us during performative spaces. These experiences have led to a number of conversations, and an invitation to ourselves and similarly minded individuals, to embark on a journey we call an 'archaeology of the self'. Journaling and body-mapping exercises have been critical in this work. These critical conversations and the sharing of ideas have often lead to poetic phrases that we have captured in our collaborative archive of texts. This space is highly energizing and has led us to identify potential collaborators across disciplines. During one of these sessions we identified possible collaborative work with a colleague in endocrinology, Dr Ian Ross, whose doctoral study involved identifying hormonal stress markers. We asked him to explore possibilities for the development of a self-administered device to track stress hormones. Ian's first response to me was in jest, *"Elelwani, now you are pushing the envelope. Medical technology is for doctors to diagnose patients, not for patients to self-understand"*. The development of the device is now at an advanced stage. In the meantime we continue with self-exploration, growing a community of practice, exploring potential research questions and finding innovative ways to fund a number of related research initiatives.

*Dance*

Normally dance is used as means of presentation and representation, and seldom as a specific means of data collection in arts-related research. Boydell (2011) documented the way in which dance was used as a form of communication with young people who had experienced their first episode of psychosis. A multiple case study approach was adopted, which examined pathways to mental health care involving interviews with 60 young people and parents, general practitioners, friends, psychiatrists, teachers and case managers. Documents and observations were also used to collect data to understand how young people sought help. Findings indicated that there was a difficulty in identifying psychosis. Concerns were also expressed by young people about stereotypes of mental illness, which prevented them from sharing their experiences and getting the correct support. Boydell suggests that:

> To take a subject such as psychosis and a form such as dance and combine them, viewing a phenomenon through both the scientific and the artistic lens, has the potential to intensify the strength and depth of meaning (Blumenfeld-Jones,1995). The choreographic process is one of sorting, sifting, editing, forming, making, and remaking—fundamentally an act

103

of discovery, an interpretation of a written text (Cancienne & Snowber, 2003). The dancer can capture an embodied understanding, an indication of the indescribable, unknowable elements of lived experience. Dancing the data induces different ways of knowing and understanding and presents a possibility for capturing the particularity and the universality of a person's experience. (Boydell, 2011)

However, we suggest there a number of issues that need to be considered when using dance in arts-related research:

– Whether it is important to choose to choreograph movement that is largely literal and represent words and phrases from interview data, or to use metaphors and symbolism
– The extent to which co-creation and performance can represent both individual and collective performance effectively, and in a way that is representative of both
– Whether it is possible to reach and manage collective agreement informally or whether some kind of formal contact is required between participants, performers and creator of the data and the work
– The extent to which it is possible to balance representation, personal engagement and the need for rigour in research.

However, when using dance in arts-related research it is also important to consider that it, like theatre and other forms of performance, is an important means both of presentation and also of introducing questions. For example, the ways the viewer encounters and experiences the spectacle can inform the reinterpretation of data as it is performed. This cycle of data collection, interpretation and (re)interpretation becomes a constant iterative cycle, which may be challenging for researchers and performers alike.

*Youth Work*

The education literature is replete with examples investigating the contribution of the arts to young people's lives; this includes how the arts have been linked to higher education achievement (DeMoss and Morris, 2002). For example, arts-related pedagogy has contributed to developing students' critical creative thinking and to enhance performance in non-academic subjects such as maths and science (Ellen et al., 2013; Bequette and Bequette, 2012). The use of poetry and Spoken Word programmes have been therapeutic experiences, which have led to overcoming shyness, increased self-confidence and self-esteem and the development of improved literate identities (Weinstein, 2010). In other examples, participation in community youth arts programmes has resulted in enhancing social and mental well-being of at-risk young people (Wood et al., 2013); developing skills and capacities in preparing students for life and work, including persistence, leadership, and collaboration (Weinstein, 2010; Kang Song & Gammel, 2011); creative thinking (Heath & Roach,

1999); problem solving (Rostan, 2010); motivation (Catterall and Chapleau, 1999; Rostan, 2010); and empathy (Catterall and Chapleau, 1999).

Levy and Weber (2011) both art educators and arts-based researchers, worked with teenage girls to share their views of being young mothers using data gathered from digital photography, art and video used during workshop sessions. The young participants re-framed, re-presented and discussed their own understandings of issues in their lives. Eight young women volunteered reflecting a mix of ethnicity and facing challenges such as poverty, abuse and growing up in foster care. The participants also kept mixed media process journals in order to consider the self-reflexive and autobiographical nature of the inquiry process. Central to the inquiry was how the researchers worked with the young women in the meaning-making process, as the presentation of their work was viewed as an essential part of the project by the young people involved. The project culminated in a large exhibition of the project work where the participants' family, friends, community representatives and health care providers attended. Their interpreted work; an exhibit, a film screening and website, revealed the courage, determination, intelligence and also at times the despair experienced by these young people in their lives. Whilst the workshop sessions had been emotionally challenging and the self-study painful at times, the participants acknowledged the work produced for the exhibit was a source of pride and accomplishment, and an important occasion to have their views and voices present, including their love for their children.

In another example, Conrad and Campbell (2008) used Popular Theatre; applied theatre using drama-based activities, to incite exploration, and as a method for education in a six-month study with a group of adolescent boys at a young offender facility in Alberta, Canada:

The focus of the study was to engage with the youth in a process that valued them as producers of knowledge. Popular Theatre was used to engage the boys in exploring their practice experiences, both prior to and during incarceration, and in envisioning their future goals. The boys used their experiences to enter into dialogue with the researchers about life as they saw it. They also made use of improvisations, play, image theatre and forum theatre work for considering other realities, making use of graffiti writing and drawing and hip hop music. This fictionalised form provides a space for safe exploration whilst enabling a distance that permits participants to contribute what they chose. As the institutional environment restricted what the boys could meaningfully contribute to decision-making, the findings from the study were disseminated using performance ethnography focussing on the themes and issues raised by the participants in relation to the institutional context, oppressive structures and the young men's processes of identity construction. The researchers took on the roles of the boys, re-enacting the dramas they had created. The researchers also shifted role to

*Continued*

focus on those of the prison staff and police guards. In addition, images from the graffiti including a music selection chosen by the boys, were used. The findings offered a self-conscious construction or fictionalised re-presentation of the inquiry, which was inherently subjective and open to multiple interpretations, portraying the creative process, evoking powerful emotion, representing the non-discursive as well as the researchers' struggles of being involved and witnessing the participants' experiences.

The performance was presented at several conferences and the script sent to the prison authority (to whom the researchers were ultimately accountable). The response to the work by the prison authorities was one of outrage! The researchers clearly presented significant issues raised by the boys. Nonetheless the researchers continued to advocate on behalf of the boys, making known to public audiences what they had heard, in order to achieve positive impact and social change for the community of participants.

The arts capitalise on the emotions, the ability to experience emotionally life at school, in a youth detention centre, in a community. The world revealed through film, theatre and arts installations can display qualities otherwise hidden.

Whilst research into the use of art as a tool for learning and development is widespread, studies often adopt the use of qualitative methodologies with methods such as interviews and observations, and quantitative design, particularly with the use of surveys, as a means to address research questions. Research about how the arts are being used as a way of exploring learning and social wellbeing, *using arts-related methodology* is less visible in the literature.

As seen in both examples, above, despite the challenges and constraints often involved in accessing young people's experiences, arts-related inquiry offers a powerful means of enabling young people to express themselves, and to challenge the perspectives held by those viewing the work. Arts-related research with youth reflects the need for diversity in stories to be shared and from a range of perspectives.

*Leadership*

Leadership development in higher education and management programs has seen an increasing range of 'arts-based' approaches being adopted such as experiencing leadership by engaging with Shakespeare's plays, painting the organisation's 'culture', and conducting symphony orchestras as a way to better understand collaborative processes. Although such ideas and techniques searching for novelty and creativity in managing and organising are expanding, there is limited empirical research being conducted into such leadership approaches. Yet the contribution of even small scale studies reflects a renewal of organisational thinking and development which is exciting and dynamic, as illustrated in the examples below:

Taylor and Ladkin (2009; 2012) have conducted research into the use of arts-based methods for development change in organisations, revealing a number of observed benefits related to leadership. Their studies have used techniques in which art is used by managers to represent aspects of themselves or their organisations. For example, Lego was used to build a three-dimensional representation of the organisation's strategy, and film was used to enable managers to gain insight or increase knowledge of key issues about culture and leadership.

During the act of making, doing, observing and creating, leadership is expereinced in an aesthetic, bodily way; a sensing activity whereby management concepts and leadership styles and approaches can be explored from alternate and often dislocated perpectives. Thus particpant understanding around leadership is constructed not only as an intellectual activity, but one that is also expressed through the senses (for example, Ladkin, 2008; Ladkin and Taylor, 2010).

Sutherland (2012) also explored the experiential learning processes inherent with arts-based methodologies in his research into management and leadership development. His work describes how use of the arts in learning environments enables such spaces to become 'aesthetic workspaces,' where participants can engage in 'aesthetic reflexivity' and create memories which can inform their future leadership practice. For example, Sutherland gathered 24 essays by Executive MBA students about their experiences of a one day master class into leadership development. The class required students to listen to a lecture on the 'performative aspects' of leadership delivered by an experienced musician and conductor. Following this the participants interacted with a professional choir *with* the conductor. The participants sat with the choir, amidst the singers, and were encouraged to observe the shared, social interactional aspects of leadership. During the musical program, the conductor encouraged the students to take turn to conduct the choir, who were singing a mixture of regional folk music and classical works. Despite raising anxiety, all the student participants had a go at conducting. The findings revealed how the use of a novel space and art form changed the notion of classroom and learning, which for some student participants was viewed as an experience they 'would never forget' and referred to it 'like being in heaven'.

The aesthetic learning space thus:

– Prompted a shift in the students' action and orientation
– Disrupted the students' expectations of themselves
– Created disjunction in the students' ability to understand what was going on
– Was uncomfortable

– Compelled students into processes of contemplation, questioning and discussion
– Developed the students' embodied experience of self and leadership
– Prompted ideas for future action

In another example, Kayrouz (2013) focused on the use of space and aesthetic perspective when he was employed as an artist-in-residence in a health insurance company which was dealing with a merger and the relocation of staff:

Approximately 500 people worked in the organisation. To address the concerns and uncertainty the management and staff were experiencing around organisational change, Kayrouz presented the management team with a scale model of an art installation.

The installation itself was to be positioned in the new work premises, be 10 metres high, and composed of small 150 x 150 cm canvases which staff would paint. Following two workshops for all staff arranged in groups of 15 – 20, the concepts of uncertainty, diversity and communication were explored through short exercises involving various aspects of painting or drawing facilitated by the artist. The first workshop was compulsory for all staff but the second could be attended voluntarily, with the company leaving open the choice to contribute a painting. Just over 300 people contributed to the final installation. Kayroux provided technical help and critique but encouraged peers to support one another. The resulting artworks were of very high quality, surprising both the staff and the artist.

Positioned in the strong light of an outside glass wall, the scale and presence of the installation was impressive. The CEO unveiled it, on a work day, in front of all the management team and staff. The art work was a metaphor for the whole organisation. The project and installation had created an energy and momentum and offered space and opportunity for staff concerns to be voiced and reflected upon in distinct ways. Whilst the project met with resistance, with some participants initially struggling to understand how 'art' would make a difference to them in their work situation, the shift occurred when the staff were exposed to the artistic experience itself, which was viewed by participants as being successful enough to modify their preconceptions. Overall the project proved valuable in creating a positive culture within the company, with staff sharing how the project had been rewarding and relevant to their work situation.

*Law*

In the final example, we turn to the field of law and how arts-related inquiry has been used to promote new ways of approaching students' ability to grasp complex subject matter.

What is evident in the examples presented is how capabilties are developed that can be applied in learning, development and organisational settings.

*Author Reflection*
**Maks Del Mar,** Senior Lecturer in Law and Philosophy, Queen Mary University London, UK

I am a legal scholar – with a principal research interest in legal theory – who has sought to draw on the arts, in particular visual and dramatic arts, in researching and teaching law. Legal scholarship and legal education are overwhelmingly text-dominated. It is arguably only relatively recently, in the last decade, that legal scholars (more collectively, rather than just the lone individual here and there) have turned to the arts, especially the visual arts to theorise about law.

My own first involvement with arts-led legal research was as one of the founders of an AHRC Network on 'Beyond Text in Legal Education'. There, we worked primarily with a visual artist and a gallery, investigating the possibility of both appreciating and making art for teaching legal professional ethics. Although this was a success in many ways (it led to a 2-volume collection of essays with Ashgate, published in 2013), I myself felt that we didn't get close enough in that project to the technical, unique aspects of legal practice – we didn't get our hands dirty enough with the details of the law. This may have been because we were learning too many new and interesting things from the artists – and as a result neglected to translate what we were learning from the arts so as to address the concerns of legal practice. Of course, there were positives in that, for the project was in part about transforming certain ethically problematic practices within legal practice. But overall, I felt more of a dialogue was needed between the artists and the lawyers: in particular, we the lawyers had to do a better job explaining the technical processes of legal reasoning to the artists.

My most recent project therefore attempted to rectify what I perceived as a lack of dialogue. Over a period of 1 year, I worked closely with a visual artist and an actress, meeting regularly throughout the year for full 5-8 hours days. Before each meeting, I prepared discussion papers, but the real work was done in the meetings themselves, during which we crafted exercises (based roughly on artistic processes) that more clearly met the learning outcomes in the law school. During those meetings, we were not only crafting exercises – we often used them to assist with our discussions – e.g. I would sketch or map out certain areas of contract law we were using as examples, and we would try out a particular exercise and see whether we ourselves felt it worked. I was amazed as to how much, as a result of those meetings, I changed how I was explaining (and also how I understood) certain features of legal reasoning, and I think the artist and actress were also amazed as to how many new versions of processes they were used to we came up with. Key here, then, was that there were research benefits for both of us: I was coming up with new insights about legal reasoning, and they

*Continued*

were coming up with new kinds of processes with new kinds of applications. It wasn't just a case of me saying to them: this is what I want to achieve, can you please build it and make it possible. It was a genuine dialogue and collaboration, which was transformative for both of us.

In terms of that project, we ended up running four 3-hour workshops for students and staff – with really positive feedback each time. Each workshop was accompanied by a detailed 'schedule' (each about 20 pages long), with descriptions of the activities side by side with learning outcomes, and also discussion points. I continue to draw on these schedules in my current research on understanding legal reasoning: what is interesting is just how fruitful it has been to theorise about legal reasoning by thinking about how one would teach it in arts-driven, non-traditional, non-text-dominated ways.

By way of illustration, here is an example of an activity we crafted. A key learning outcome of our workshop on reading cases was to assist the students to pay close attention to the facts that were described in the case and how they were described. In order to facilitate this, we drew on a technique from the dramatic arts, commonly employed by actors in first-stage rehearsals: we got the students to walk around the room, reading a blown-up segment of the text out loud, changing direction with each punctuation mark. Students had never previously read any text of a case out loud (aside from a brief quote they might mention in class) – this in itself was an experience that, because of its novelty value, allowed them to pay closer attention to what was said and how it was said. Further, and more strikingly, the physical element of changing direction with each punctuation mark was important, for it allowed students to kinesthetically experience the rhythm of the judges' reasoning: one of the students said after the exercise that she noticed

*Continued*

that the judge would use short and crisp sentences when he was confident about some factual finding, and long and wandering sentences when he was less sure. In the research process, we considered a number of different versions of this 'walk-n-read' exercise – eventually adding the important component of changing direction with each punctuation mark when we realized (after we performed the exercise ourselves!) that a vital aspect of how the facts are described in a case is the kind and degree of use of punctuation marks.

What the case studies have illustrated is the diverse engagement across media that occurs when artist, art form and artistic process are combined with person, subject, and disciplinary knowledge. Arts-related approaches may not always be experienced as positive and may uncover unexpected challenges and problems within disciplinary contexts, as illustrated through the ways in which viewers may respond to what is portrayed (Conrad and Campbell, 2008). Yet the aim of arts-related inquiry is not to present answers or offer solutions, but to generate questions to 'stimulate problem formulation' (Barone & Eisner, 2012:171). What is also evident is that further research is required to examine the longer-term impact of arts-related inquiry and learning and development in the disciplines; including research which can follow participants back into their contexts and fields of practice.

## CONCLUSION

This chapter has considered arts-related research across diverse disciplines and complex contexts. Case study examples illustrate the benefits which can occur when artists, art forms and the artistic process coalesce as part of research practice with other disciplines and practices, such as health, leadership, medicine and law. What is apparent is that when the arts are used as research tools for learning and development, disciplinary boundaries are reduced. For staff, students, researchers and arts-related researchers subject knowledge and pedagogic knowledge merge and are transformed.

# DIGITAL ART(S) AND DIGITAL MÉTISSAGE

## INTRODUCTION

This chapter explores more recent forms of art, such as digital art, and also examines the new and different ways in which arts-related research is combining new media in order to undertake research, such as (digital) métissage and digital a/r/tography. The chapter begins by delineating a/r/tography, digital arts, and digital métissage, and providing exemplars of work in these areas. The rest of the chapter outlines ways in which arts-related research might be undertaken and how it may be adopted and adapted for inquiry in and for the future. It suggests one of the main challenges for those undertaking digital arts-related research is the liquidity of arts and digital media and the potential overlap between these and the research approach adopted.

## A/R/TOGRAPHY

As mentioned in earlier chapters, A/r/tography, as defined by Irwin and de Cosson (2004), is a form of practice-based research located in both the arts and education that offers a means of researching the world to enhance understanding. We refer to it again now as it helps to frame and link some of the newer arts-related research and practices we discuss below. A/r/tography is delineated by the artist/researcher/ teacher, as the frame of reference through which art practice is explored:

- The Artist en-acts and embodies creative and critical inquiry;
- The Researcher acts in relation to the culture of the research community;
- The Teacher re-acts in ways that involve others in artistic inquiry and educational outcomes (Sullivan, 2006)

A/r/tographers have interests in education, schooling, community and culture – their focus is on developing the practitioner-researcher capable of conducting insightful inquiry (Sullivan, 2006). This approach is seen as having a robust focus of non-linguistic forms of artistic engagement, together with a resilient element of reflexive engagement, so that its adoption makes use of the creative and critical features of artistic knowing in the context of research.

More recently a/r/tography has been described as a process of inquiring in the world through the process of art making, in which the components of writing and art are woven in ways that indicate that they are interconnected and relate to one another. Works of this sort are positioned and enacted as exchanges between text and art in ways that bring inquiry, identity, metaphor, interrogation and shared inquiry together. In some contexts a/r/tography is used to investigate teaching and learning in order that the artist/researcher/teacher can examine their practices. The arguments for this approach

> ... stem from a belief that if forms of arts-based research are to be taken seriously as emerging fields within educational research, then perhaps they need to be understood as methodologies in their own right, not as extensions of qualitative research. This entails moving beyond the use of existing criteria that exists for qualitative research and toward an understanding of interdisciplinarity not as a patchwork of different disciplines and methodologies but as a loss, a shift, or a rupture where in absence, new courses of action unfold. (Springgay et al., 2005: 898)

We suggest that whilst this is a challenging stance, the danger of such an approach is that the research is dislocated from any kind of philosophical position. Adopting a research approach that fits with the research paradigm at the outset of the project will make the research design stronger, and doing so will enable a researcher to develop a clearer argument for the approach and methods they have adopted. Thus it is important to consider that researchers position themselves in relation to their philosophies, whether consciously or unconsciously, as they consider how to undertake a given study. Therefore we argue for the importance of being explicit about the choice of philosophies that underpin the research, even when using a/r/tography. However, perhaps it is important to reconnect too with the roots of a/r/tography, which has been located in ethnography. Ethnography comes from the Greek, *ethnos*, translated as 'folk,' and is thus the study of people, cultures and values. Although there are many different views about what counts as ethnography, it is an approach that requires intensive fieldwork to gain a detailed and comprehensive view of a social group and its setting. Therefore it is a sound fit with a/r/tography.

## DIGITAL ART(S)

In the changing landscapes of arts-related research and how digital media are being used for learning and research, it is important to examine how 'the digital' is being used in art practice as well as assessing its impact on research. Digital art is a term used to describe contemporary art that uses digital media methods for the creation, representation or as a central component of the creative process. Digital media has transformed activities such as sculpture and painting whilst at the same time new forms of art have emerged, such as digital installation art. Various names have been used to refer to artistic work that uses digital media, such as new media art, computer art and multimedia art. Digital art is also often referred to as new media art and has been shaped by the rise, shifts and changes in technology. Lister *et al.* (2009: 10) suggest that the term 'new' was used to indicate a shift in the ways in which media were produced, received, reproduced and shared. However, we draw on Savin-Baden's concept of new media which argues that it should be seen as:

> … media at the intersections of books, television, and radio with interactive media and social networking. Such media are seen as new in that they are not tied to any context, platform or situation, but are associated with culture, identity, belonging and voice. In the context of this book they encompass informal and formal learning settings, as well as those at the interstices of both. (Savin-Baden, 2015: Chapter 6)

Those in the digital art field argue that if work is to be classed as digital art, it must be both valuable from an aesthetic view as well as original, so that the art is not a mere copy of reality, but proffers an underlying message.

There is now a wide range of digital art, and while some forms have introduced new issues or forms of interruption, others are extensions of more traditional work. For example, digital installation art has resulted in a shift in the way that spatial components are seen in galleries – so that spaces become new sites of interaction, that in some cases cross spatial and temporal borders, as exemplified by the work of Upton, mentioned in Chapter 1. Other work, by film makers such as Stogner, challenges us to look at the spaces and the interstices of what counts as technology and what does not, and the ways in which such explorations challenge us to see spaces differently.

Stogner (2013) suggests that today's media is changing cultural narratives and that we now have an explosive rise of story telling technologies: the medium is instant messaging:

> Today's narratives ebb and flow in a sea of continual action and reaction. Frequently, there is no beginning, middle, and end. No plot. No heroic archetypal characters. No narrator. The public-at-large is contributor, critic, and curator. (Stogner, 2013)

*Participatory narratives* involve the process of creating, critiquing, and curating so that everyday heroes create their own quests and journeys. In practice people share fragments of their stories, photos, virtual exhibitions and videos. An extension of participatory narratives is, Stogner suggests, purposeful participation, whereby technologies are used to create shared opportunities that add value to the shared artefacts and the users themselves. She cites the interactive installation, From Memory to Action, at the U.S. Holocaust Memorial Museum in Washington D.C., which enables users to watch video testimonies about genocide, select stories of personal interest, and share them.

*Collective narratives* are where people engage with others who are disparate across time and space. The authorial voice is formed by the contributions of many, who in turn create aggregated mega stories. An example is the Question Bridge project www.questionbridge.com, which defines itself as a collective trans-media project that is creating a 'mega-logue' among black men in the U.S.

*Mobile narratives* are where narratives are told through whatever sources people choose to use on the move, whether through apps or superimposing video, poems and animation in any environment. An example of this is 'Gradually Melt the Sky,' which creates a performance event 'at once cosmic and mundane, an action painting and a protest' with AR to 'overlay, intervene and challenge the physical world' (Skwarek, & Pappenheimer, 2011).

## FORMS OF DIGITAL ARTS

Digital arts have been seen as a means of being able to capture and create art. More recently, they have also been seen as a means of both data collection and data representation in arts-related research. Digital art includes a whole range of works and methods, from digital storytelling to crowd sourcing (in which large numbers of people across demographics contribute information and knowledge via the Internet). In terms of arts-related research it is important to locate the digital arts, many of which can be linked to collaborative modes of inquiry. Since the emergence of action research there has been a rising interest in collaborative approaches to research, resulting in increasing numbers of collaborative approaches being carried out, which in turn has led advocates of these approaches in many and varied directions. Collaborative approaches focus highly on cooperative and collaborative working in order to bring about action and change. Collaborative researchers tend to adopt the philosophical positions of either constructionism or constructivism. They tend to be explicit about their personal position and research tends to focus on problem-solving and the expressed concept of change, with there always being a strong sense of working with shared values.

### Interactive Art

Although interactive art was first displayed in the 1960s, its real growth was during the 1980s in the areas of experimental art and technology, that occurred in the fields of music, performance, film and the visual arts. Since then there has been a shift in focus so that interactive art is both important in terms of the way the art in appears in and through technology, and also in the way it performs. Interactive arts are seen (following Candy & Edmonds, 2002), based on Cornock and Edmonds (1973) as being:

- Static – whereby the object neither changes nor responds to its context, examples of this would be paintings or photographs in a gallery
- Dynamic-Passive – where the object changes through an internal mechanism specified by the artist, such as light or temperature, and the viewer is a passive recipient of the activity that is performed.

- Dynamic-Interactive – this is similar to the dynamic passive category but here the viewer has an active role in influencing the changes in the art object. For example, walking over lights might produce sounds so that the work 'performs' differently according to how the viewer acts.
- Dynamic-Interactive (Varying) – this combines dynamic-passive and dynamic-interactive with an additional component whereby the art is modified. Thus the artist updates the art object that is learning from the experiences of interaction, so that the performance of the art object varies.

Thus in the case of interactive art the role of the artist requires both the creation of the work, and also the decision about how the relationship will occur between the work and its viewers, and finally the ways these will be used and portrayed as research. Interactive art tends to cross over into the areas of digital installation art and vidding, which pose similar challenges about the relationship between the work, the portrayal and the research, as discussed in Chapter 5.

*Digital Installation Art*

This comprises a wide range of activities such as projects, interactive videos, virtual worlds interactions, and installations. For example, projection techniques are used to create immersive environments so that audiences will feel engaged and immersed. Some of these installations are portable and can be reconfigured to accommodate different presentation spaces, so that they might mix media, and might be static, dynamic or interactive. Morrison et al (2010) explored design considerations in mixed reality art works, suggesting that in designing for performativity it is important to focus on the potential actions that emerge from participants in a construction environment. He presents *Dislocation,* which is a gallery based installation in which visual and auditory displays, combined with audience locational data, create the impression that realistic virtual characters inhabit the same physical space as the audience. They argue that there is now a need for a mode of performative design:

> This is one that entails other approaches to design research (e.g. critical, discursive, participatory) in conducting research by design. However, a more extended view on performative design research centred on practices geared towards active participative engagement – affectively, expressively and communicatively – which may be co-partnered with the emergent, tentative and even ludic actions on the part of participants for whom the design for performativity becomes material for their own mediated meaning making. In performative design terms, on the part of participants in mixed reality installations, this may entail the experience and reflection on being 'the Other' and processes of negotiating 'dislocation' and the effects of engagement in realising designs for performativity (Morrison et al, 2010: 140)

Work by Chafer at Coventry University blends realities by using avatars projected into theatre productions, as well as performing traditional theatre in Second Life. For example in, 2008, two scenes from Hamlet were performed live in a recreation of the Globe Theatre in SecondLife(TM). The performance was mediated through voice, through the representation of the avatars, through gestures and through the positioning of the avatars within the stage space. His work and research includes Alice in WonderSLand (Chafer, 2010) and combining with the University of South Australia on *Staging Second Life*, whereby students transposed a virtual world into a theatrical setting and were examined on their experiences of learning through these media (Fewster et al., 2010).

*Vidding and Produsage*

Vidding is where content is refashioned or recreated in order to present a different perspective, usually based on music videos and television programmes. The purpose of vidding is to critique, re-present and explore an aspect of the original media. Such an example of this is an Anime music video (AMV) that is usually fan made and comprises a range of clips from a variety of sources such films, songs and promotional trailers. These amateur videos are posted on sites such as YouTube and AnimeMusicVideos.org and with the advent of networked media, interests can be supported by platforms such as LiveJournal, Tumblr, Pinterest, and sites devoted and designed for specific interest groups such as DeviantArt, Ravelry, or fantasy sports leagues (Ito et al., 2013: 64). Although vidding is a complex and highly skilled activity, like many other digital activities its sharing and learning is important only to those in the vidding community, and in the main not to those in other learning arenas. Both vidding and produsage are practices that intricately combine research and practice in ways that are almost seamless, as Turk (2010: 89) argues:

> Vidders thus position themselves simultaneously as fans, filmmakers, and critics. Vids express what vidders find important in the source narrative, which characters, relationships, stories and subtexts they find most interesting and rewarding to examine. A vid represents a close reading, and like any close reading it is selective: vidders can retain or subvert the original story, foreground a minor story element or character, excise the parts of the story that displease them, or create a new story altogether. Vids are therefore opportunities to resist as well as reinscribe visual narratives.

It could be argued that traditional academic practices erode or prevent creative learning practices in young people, by failing to acknowledge the playful practices involved in the use of new technologies. The result is a form of liquid media – a sense of engaging with, recreating, redeveloping and representing that which is continually on the move. Such liquid media are a shift away from what was previously seen as a relatively straight forward mashup, something created by combining elements from two or more sources, which generally originated from music but moved into films and more recently digital media. However, what is also important is the notion of produsage. Bruns (2008) argues for produsage, which is the collaborative and continuous building and extending of existing content in pursuit of further improvement (Bruns, 2008; Bruns & Schmidt, 2012), which is characterized by:

– Community-based activities – produsage proceeds from the assumption that the community as a whole, if sufficiently large and varied, can contribute more than a closed team of producers, however qualified they may be.
– Fluid roles – produsers participate as is appropriate to their personal skills, interests, and knowledges; this changes as the produsage project proceeds.
– Unfinished artefacts – content artefacts in produsage projects are continually under development, and therefore always unfinished; their development follows evolutionary, iterative, palimpsestic paths.
– Common property, individual merit – contributors permit (non-commercial) community use, adaptation and further development of their intellectual property, and are rewarded by the status capital they gain through this process.

It is not clear how the blurred edges around particular practices are managed, engineered and contended with, in terms of how people undertake activities such as archiving, annotating, appropriating, mashing up, recirculating, interacting, responding, critiquing, remixing and participating across diverse social and traditional media. However, digital arts such as vidding, produsage and gaming introduce new notions of space that are both creative and speculative. For example, Jarvinen (2001; 2010) suggests that the aesthetics and archaeologies of online gaming take the form of a spectacle, and blur the boundaries of play, narrative, space, entertainment and art. He suggests that games are a form of popular art, since they are located between the aesthetics of the moving image and the aesthetics of the environment. Thus it would seem that risk and precariousness, along with new conceptions of space, are at the heart of digital arts.

*Computer-Generated Visual Media*

These media comprise 2D and 3D visual art. This can be in the form of 2D computer graphics, which reflect what an artist might draw using a pencil and a piece of paper, but the image is on the computer screen and the drawing instrument might be a tablet stylus or a mouse. In 3D computer graphics, the screen becomes a window into a virtual environment, and objects are arranged in order to be captured, as in the form of a photograph, by the computer. These 3D graphics are created though designing imagery ranging from three-dimensional objects, games and special effects, as well as film and television scenes.

An example of this is visual aesthetics, such as the creation of art that introduces a sense of life though movement. An illustration of this is 'Rain room at the curve' where a sense of life is instilled though simulating something that is natural. This work explores both the response to the art and peoples' responses within the immersive environment, thus transcending art and data collection. Random International's Rain Room is a 100 square metre field of falling water for visitors to walk through and experience how it might feel to control the rain. When they enter visitors hear the sound of water before discovering falling droplets respond to their presence and movement. Random International said:

> Rain Room is the latest in a series of projects that specifically explore the behaviour of the viewer and viewers: pushing people outside their comfort zones, extracting their base auto-responses and playing with intuition. Observing how these unpredictable outcomes will manifest themselves, and the experimentation with this world of often barely perceptible behaviour and its simulation is our main driving force. (Barbican press release, 02/03/13)

A further example is the work of the English artist David Hockney, who explained:

> The computer is a useful tool. Photoshop is a computer tool for picture making. It in effect allows you to draw directly in a printing machine, one of its many uses. One draws with the colours the printing machine has, and the printing machine is one anyone can have. They are now superior to any other kinds of printing, but because it is very slow, of limited commercial appeal.

> I used to think the computer was too slow for draughtsmen. You had finished a line, and the computer was 15 seconds later, an absurd position for someone drawing, but things have improved, and it now enables one to draw very freely and fast with colour. There are advantages and disadvantages to anything new in mediums for artists, but the speed allowed here with colour is something new, swapping brushes in the hand with oil or water colour takes time. These prints are made by drawing and collage, they exist either in the computer or on a piece of paper, they were made for printing, and so will be printed. They are not photographic reproductions. My idea is to make then in small editions between 7 and 25. (Hockney. November 2008)

In 2011 an exhibition was staged at the Royal Ontario Museum in Toronto presenting the playful drawings of Hockney, produced with and for the iPhone and iPad. Hockney first shared his digital drawings with friends and then he decided to make them available world wide. See Figure 8.1.

*Figure 8.1. David-Hockney-Ipad-Flower*

## Digital Story Telling

Digital story telling involves asking participants to present their point of view using images. It requires them to consider the use of their voice, the choice of music and the way the story is paced and presented. Many artist-researchers began using these new ways of representation by including narratives, poetry and photographs in traditional journal articles (for example, Park-Fuller, 2000; 2003). This approach builds on traditional storytelling and is combined with digital technology (see for example, *http://www.storycenter.org/index1.html*). A digital story is usually short, often presented in the first person and is a video-narrative created through a combination of voice, music, and still and moving images. One way of creating a digital story is to use the software that is freely downloadable, for example photostory. What is useful about this narrative form is that it can be created by anyone who has a desire to document life experience, ideas or feelings, through the use of digital media. However, as Burgess (2006) points out, with the changes in world literacy practices in terms of how media are used, it is important to consider that the use of media for research have ethical and methodological implications, as well as unresolved tensions around issues such as agency and value. Burgess (2006) used the example of digital storytelling to explore the participatory cultural studies approach to research. The advantages of it are that it is low tech, accessible, user generated and requires minimal training. Digital storytelling involves asking participants to present their point of view using images, but it also requires researchers to consider the use of their voice, their choice of music, and the way the story is paced and presented. In order to use this approach effectively for arts-related research it would be important to:

— Decide on the type of narrative approach,
— Ask participants to create their own stories
— Obtain the digital stories from the participants
— Analyse the stories using a narrative analysis framework, such as interactional analysis or performance analysis.

## DIGITAL MÉTISSAGE

Digital métissage is based on the idea of literary métissage as outlined by Hasebe-Ludt et al. (2009). Literary métissage is the process of creating stories that are braided together and rooted in history and memory, as well as being stories of be-coming. It is a form of arts-based inquiry that reaches across differences and creates collective inquisitiveness about the issues being presented and explored.

> Methodological positioning is the way in which researchers position themselves within the given methodology they have chosen. For example, researchers may adopt narrative inquiry but within it they will need to consider their relationship to participants and context, as well as the way their own biography may affect the research process.

The principle of métissage in terms of methodological positioning is that although arts-based research is not easily located as one bounded methodology, (in ways that it is often possible to do with narrative inquiry and ethnography and so on), it is possible to locate it philosophically. However, we suggest that most arts-informed approaches sit with post-modernism, constructionism and constructivism, as explained in Chapter 1. In using digital métissage all these philosophical positions along with all the genres of arts-related research (in Table 1.1) may be combined, blurred and overlaid with one another.

Thus using the concept of métissage enables researchers to use arts informed approaches in ways that are not isolated (or isolating) from mainstream research methods, but instead work across boundaries in fluid ways.

Thus literary métissage provokes engagement with dominant discourse(s) in order to challenge and change them. Digital métissage captures the idea of blurring genres, texts, histories and stories in digital formats that recognise the value and spaces between and across cultures, generations and representational forms. The notion of métissage (French meaning hybridisation or fusion) brings with it the sense of braiding so that the process of digital métissage requires co-production and co creation with participants in ways that braid data and stories.

## Co-Creation in Digital Métissage

Co creation is defined here (following Saldaña, 2010; Boydell, 2011) as a collective activity between participants, artists and researchers that attends to the processual aspects of participants' experiences. Using these forms of co creation will enable the researcher team to study the process of the creation of the assets with artists and participants, thereby enabling the process and creation of assets to produce generalizable knowledge from the empirical research findings. Thus, through collection of stories it will be possible to co create and characterize experience in ways that are both individual and collective, whilst also creating and displaying visual and emotional aspects of the stories, assets and research. The focus on 'the digital;' also recognises the importance of connectivity as a complex and contested concept, in terms of both bonding and bridging (Putnam, 2000: 22-23). Unlike Putnam's arguments, the suggestion here is that by gathering and sharing art, artefacts and stories, digital media can be used to engage with digital métissage which facilitates both bridging social capital and bonding despite differences.

---

***Author Reflection***
*Digital Métissage: Creative Braiding*
**Carl Leggo**, University of British Columbia, Canada

For a long time, I have been engaging in methods of research that can be called métissage and digital métissage, but I have not always been able to name the ways that I have pursued my research. When I joined the Department of Language and Literacy Education at the University of British Columbia in 1990, I presented myself as a poet and teacher and scholar with a keen interest in creative approaches to researching experiences of teaching and learning.

My doctoral dissertation, defended in 1989, was full of poetry and playful prose. Since the mid-1980s, I have been seeking to participate in an unfolding contemporary aesthetic which, Gregory Ulmer announced in 1984, entails 'the collapse of the distinction (opposition or hierarchy) between critical-theoretical reflection and creative practice' (p. 225). For a quarter century in my scholarship I have been pursuing diverse arts, media, and research approaches. Today with the ubiquitous proliferation of digital technologies and arts-based research, the possibilities of digital métissage are bountifully inviting.

As a poet and fiction writer, I am always seeking ways to compose stories and essays in creative performances. Digital métissage is a way of creative braiding. I have collaborated with many colleagues (2008a, 2008b, 2009, 2010), especially Erika Hasebe-Ludt and Cynthia Chambers, in processes of braiding our stories, poetry, photographs, ruminations, theorizing, and performances. As an arts-based researcher I enjoy the privilege of collaborating with colleagues and students

---

*Continued*

who are visual artists, photographers, videographers, musicians, dancers, actors, and story-tellers. Out of many creative (and often complex) collaborations, I have experimented with oral performances of texts, combining poetry with visual art, and presenting poetry in response to a dancer's movement or a musician's compositions. I have participated in dramatic performances in convention centre hallways, in grassy fields, and on proscenium stages.

When I engage with the possibilities of métissage, I explore possibilities of intersections and interjections and interconnections. I engage in digital métissage for many reasons. First, I enjoy the opportunity to engage in conversation with others where our diverse voices evoke multiplicity. Second, I enter into creative relationships full of mystery where I learn to trust that the artful process of engaging with diverse media will not master mystery but will remind us to revel in mystery. Third, digital métissage connects the mind, imagination, heart, and body in a holistic celebration of nterconnections. Fourth, digital métissage invites possibilities for radical and transformative learning. Finally, digital métissage is fun. And research ought to be fun!

I invite students to inquire creatively and interrogatively. I encourage them to take risks, to experiment with diverse discourses, and to challenge conventions, even as I have done for a long time:

> do I need to know
> where I have come
> from
> where I am going
> the whirling dervish
> of derivation & delineation
>
> perhaps I should
> make up stories
> and learn to live well
> in the places
> of métissage
>
> where stories know
> what I can't know:
> even as
> I braid
> the possibilities
> &
> the possibilities
> braid me

*Continued*

> As an artist, researcher, and teacher (I now call myself an a/r/tographer) in the academy, I have pursued my vocation with an abiding commitment to both creative discourse and critical discourse. I am steeped in the arts as a way of knowing and being and becoming. As a research process, digital métissage evokes and provokes possibilities for meaning-making, full of startling surprises.

CONCLUSION

The arts-related approaches discussed in this chapter range from the use of more traditional media creation to new and emerging methods that have a sense of the liquid. Whilst the approaches here have been discussed discretely, it is clear that there is much overlap. Yet what is central to using any of these approaches is the need to ensure that the researcher stance and the creation of the work are seen as interactive components, and that one neither takes precedence over nor subverts the other. Managing such tensions are inherent in arts-related research but perhaps more so when using diverse and overlapping (digital) media, which bring continual movement, interruption and disruption. There are a further set of challenges we face in the future, and it is to these we turn in Chapter 9.

# NEW CARTOGRAPHIES FOR ARTS-RELATED RESEARCH

## INTRODUCTION

This chapter suggests that arts-related research needs to take up a new critical stance and move beyond what in some instances have become traditional arts-based spaces that hark back to the 1980s. What we suggest is that arts-related research can be philosophically located in ways that do not mean that they are locked down and tightly bounded. Instead we provide examples and suggestions of ways that arts-related research can be positioned that reflect diversity and complexity and rigour. The chapter delineates different ways of formulating arts-related research, whilst also recognizing the overlaps between the different methodologies suggested.

## CHALLENGING ISSUES

Haseman (2006) has gone so far as to argue that there is a need to introduce a new paradigm, a performative paradigm, which is suited to creative arts research. He argues:

> performative research represents a move which holds that practice is the principal research activity – rather than *only* the practice of performance – and sees the material outcomes of practice as all-important representations of research findings in their own right Haseman (2006: 103).

Thus he suggests that this is distinct from qualitative and quantitative paradigms and can be represented as follows:

*Table 9.1. Performative research (Haseman 2006: 102)*

| Quantitative research | Qualitative research | Performative research |
|---|---|---|
| 'the activity or operation of expression something as a quantity or amount – for example, in numbers, graphs, or formulas' (Schwandt, 2001:215) | Refers to 'all forms of social inquiry that rely primarily on qualitative data, i.e. nonnumeric data in the form of words' (Schwandt, 2001:213) | Expressed in nonnumeric data, but in forms of symbolic data other than words in discursive text. These include material forms of practice, of still and moving images, of music and sound, of live action and digital code. |
| The scientific method | Multi-method | Multi-method led by practice |

Whilst we believe this is an interesting and useful suggestion, it needs to be recognized that researchers will always operate in some kind of framework. Further, Haseman holds a rather naive stance, which takes into account neither the diversity of the qualitative methodologies available nor the philosophical stances inherent in each one. Much of what Haseman suggests can be located in one or other of the qualitative approaches. Furthermore, it is rare that any research operates outside a framework and, as Popper (1970) argued, all thought (and presumably action and experience), takes place within some kind of framework, although we are not forever confined to this framework. Barnett (1994) has argued that Popper avoided the issue that the practical rules of a particular framework forbid an examination of the framework itself; to do so would run counter to the very nature of the framework. Thus by deconstructing one framework that is the basis of the discipline, other related frameworks thereby become problematic as all the other connecting boundaries become problematic. Perhaps the overarching question that needs to be asked relates not to whether a performative paradigm is needed but:

– What assumptions are being made and supported when taking up a researcher stance?
– What is coded in and coded out of performance, interpretation and representation?

For example, in phenomenology the researcher stance is invariably coded out (bracketed) but equally a performative paradigm may code in practice but code out theories and philosophies that could inform the research. Thus it is important to recognize how different paradigms help and hinder what it is that is being researched and the ways that different findings are represented:

– Positivism — knowledge exists and it is expected that properties and relations may be discovered through the scientific method (quantitative)
– Post-positivism — knowledge exists but it is imperfectly understandable, and it may be possible through trial and error, to discover what is false (quantitative and some forms of qualitative research such as pragmatic approaches, phenomenology and grounded theory)
– Critical theory — positive knowledge exists and may be discovered through historical approaches, and understanding society through the different disciplines of the social sciences
– Pragmatism — reality exists for individuals, but knowledge is seen as contextual and contingent, so that knowledge may be discovered by examining the usefulness of theory in practice.
– Phenomenology — knowledge may be discovered by exploring human experiences, since reality and knowledge reside in the mind, as the individual perceives and experiences it
– Post/critical/modern/structuralism — reality and knowledge may be found deeply embedded in structures, but human agency is problematic since there

are many truths and systems, and such systems impose linguistic codes and structures. Examining codes and structures can help researchers uncover knowledge.

– Constructionism — reality and knowledge are socially constructed; knowledge may be gained by examining the ways in which individuals co-create knowledge.
– Constructivism — reality and knowledge reside in the minds of individuals; knowledge may be uncovered by unpacking individual experiences.

Thus we suggest that perhaps there does need to be a new methodological positioning of arts-related research that locates it more distinctly both paradigmatically and methodologically. It is evident that some methodologies fit less well with arts-related research than others. To date this has largely been unacknowledged, and therefore we suggest it might be viewed as a new landscape:

## NEW CARTOGRAPHIES FOR ARTS-RELATED RESEARCH

What we mean by new cartographies is that arts-related research can be positioned within a landscape of qualitative methodologies whilst being flexible, critical and unbounded. We suggest the following possibilities:

– Arts-related narrative approaches
– Arts-related case study
– Arts-related action research
– Arts-related ethnography
– Arts-related evaluation
– Arts-related collaborative inquiry
– Arts-related pragmatic research
– Arts-related phenomenology
– Arts-related grounded theory

### Arts-related Narrative Approaches

The focus in arts-related narrative approaches is to examine the meaning in stories, so that researchers suggest people create themselves and reality through narrative and the arts. The origins of narrative as an approach to research can be seen in the biographical interpretive method as developed by German sociologists, for example, to produce accounts of the lives of Holocaust survivors and Nazi soldiers (Wengraf, 2001). Narrative approaches generally focus on developing understanding through an exploration of story, interpretation and discourse (Leggo, 2008), with a focus on the story for both data collection and presentation. Stories tend to have context, characters, plot, place, turning points and resolutions. Researchers examine and use these conventions when presenting the story, often bringing to the fore the experiences of the participants, at times at the expense of more conventional manuscript formats.

129

Hollway and Jefferson (2000) have suggested that four principles facilitate the production of the interviewee's meaning, which we have adapted here:

1. Use open-ended questions: 'Tell me about your stories of creating a play.'
2. Elicit stories: 'Relate examples of creating an artwork that is particularly memorable.'
3. Avoid 'why' questions – as these tend to encourage intellectualisation and can be threatening.
4. Follow up using respondents' ordering and phrasing: 'You said working in a different artist medium felt complicated', can you tell me some more about that?

However, we suggest that when using narrative inquiry it is important that the researcher is both able to ask questions that elicit stories, and also that they are able to position themselves so that stories, including their own, can be analysed effectively. Stories constructed by the narrator (written, oral and even film) have been used by anthropologists and sociologists who label their work as ethnography. Yet we increasingly believe that the distinction between different types of narrative inquiry tends to signal overlap between methodology and the artistic process.

---

### *Example*

Estrell, K. and Forinash, M. (2007) Perspectives Narrative Inquiry and Arts-Based Inquiry: Multinarrative *Journal of Humanistic Psychology* 47 (3) 376-383

This article introduces narrative inquiry and arts-based research methods and provides a discussion of the applicability of these methods for exploring the marginalized, controversial, and disruptive perspectives that have often been lost in more traditional research methodologies. Narrative and arts-based approaches to research offer the possibility of disruption to the dominant discourses within theory and research. In addition, they also provide an avenue toward reconciliation. The authors explore how these two research approaches can be used. Philosophical groundwork for their application to the work of conflict resolution and practices of reconciliation is offered.

---

*Arts-related Case Study*

Case study tends to be used to examine the relationship between people and structures, in which they work, live and learn. For many researchers case study is adopted because it is an approach in which the dynamics of interaction are seen as the starting point for research. This approach is generally seen as emerging from the Chicago School interactionists in the early 1900s, and more recently from scholars in the field of education such as Adelman et al. (1980), Yin (1984) and Stake (1995).

Stake also used case study in educational evaluation. The difficulty with case study is that there are many types, from different philosophical roots. We suggest that arts-related case study is one that seeks to develop conceptual categories or theories in conjunction with the artistic process, so that data gathering is used for the explicit function of theorising. Findings are presented in depth, and with thick description and artistic rigour.

---

*Example*

Reingold, R. (2014) Moses' Black Wife: A Case Study Analysis of Secondary School Students' Arts-Based Projects *Journal of Jewish Education* 80, (2) 99-120

Practitioner research was conducted on Grade 10 students' arts-based projects of Numbers 12 in order to assess the value of using the arts in Jewish secondary schools. Based on interview transcripts, projects, and written statements, three themes emerged that demonstrated why teachers should use the arts in their classes. The arts provided students the opportunity to act as commentators, form personal connections to the text, and meet educational and curricular goals such as memory retention and enhanced group skills. This article provides a case study of two projects that used the same storyline in order to provide evidence for the importance of using the arts in Jewish education.

---

*Arts-related Action Research*

Action Research is generally associated with Lewin, who is seen as the 'father' of Action Research (Kemmis & McTaggart, 1988). Action research seeks to use methods through working with people and not 'doing' research on them. Savin-Baden and Major (2013) define action research as:

> *a method of qualitative research the purpose of which is to engage in problem-solving through a cyclical process of thinking, acting, data gathering and reflection.* Action Research at its heart is about changing and improving practice and understanding of practice, through a combination of systematic reflection and strategic innovation. It requires that participants be empowered and stresses the importance of leading social change. In most cases, Action Research also contains a knowledge creation element, so that understanding and theory are created through practice. (Savin-Baden and Major, 2013: 245)

Arts-related action research tends to focus on intervention, development and change that is conducted within communities and groups, and involves examining an issue systematically from the perspectives and experiences of the community members most affected by that issue. The approach focuses on the effects of the researcher's actions within a participatory community.

> **Example**
>
> Hutzel, K. E., & Kim, I. (2013). Situating an Art-based Action Research Study within Social Justice Theories. *Archives of Design Research,* 26(2) 35-53
>
> *Methods* — The paper aims to answer two main questions through the critical reflections on an art-based, action research study: (1) what does social justice look like, particularly in the arts? (2) Do arts-based, action research studies contribute to social justice for the participants? The case study is designed to use community arts as a means to empower the women (n=16) who were domestic violence survivors and homeless. Using their art works as the women's voices, an art exhibit was held to initiate civic discussions and engagement on a community level. To investigate the social impacts of community arts, audience surveys (n=74), informal and formal interviews, participatory observation, and journaling were employed as the research methods of this case study.
>
> *Results* — The collected data strongly indicates that art can be an exceptionally powerful tool for communication and healing, especially when words and discussions fall short. In addition, art appears extremely effective to elicit not only emotional but also intellectual responses among the research participants regarding the subject matter, domestic violence. In particular, the main theme that occurred from the collected data was 'mutual respect and compassion' between the women and the audience through their shared experience, the women's art exhibit. In essence, the themes of the collected evidences indicate civic friendship as the outcome of the case study that falls into the pluralistic view of social justice theories.

*Arts-related Ethnography*

Ethnography is a broad research approach that originally focussed on exploring different cultures from an anthropological perspective; it has now evolved into many different types of ethnography. However, important characteristics include the researcher:

- Seeking to understand what is 'normal' within a context.
- Being immersed in a particular field or setting for an extended period of time
- Using participant observation as a primary method so that through participating in the community it is possible to come to understand it better.
- Using in-depth and unstructured data collection
- Presenting the findings from the participants' point of view.

Researchers use ethnography to understand a day-to-day picture of a particular group, although traditional ethnography is now difficult to undertake because of the extended time and in-depth field work required to carry it out. However, recent shifts to more varied forms of ethnography have enabled it to be seen as an approach that has more utilitarian value. It is now adopted in more localised settings than earlier studies, and is commonly used in distinct geographical locations, to study marginalised and under-represented groups, such as the homeless.

---

### Example

Behar, R. (2003) Ethnography and the Book that was Lost *Ethnography* 4 (1): 15-39

This article is a meditation on the way ethnography, as a method and form of expression, has informed a range of reflexive anthropological journeys in Spain, Mexico, and Cuba. It uses a poetic sense of reflexivity to explore the embedded nature of personal experience within the ethnographic process. Borrowing the metaphor of `the lost book' from a fictional story by Agnon, the article explores the contradictory dynamic that emerges in witnessing loss and simultaneously wanting to preserve culture. Ultimately, the article urges ethnographers to pay attention to intuition, serendipity, and unexpected moments of epiphany in the quest for ethnographic ways of knowing, while encouraging ethnographers to present their findings in a wider variety of literary and artistic genres.

---

### Arts-related Evaluation

This form of evaluation takes the stance that arts-based media facilitate the portrayal of the process, learning and outcomes of evaluation. However, the use of creative arts for designing, interpreting and presenting an evaluation as a whole is still relatively underdeveloped. There are a number of central principles that can help to delineate this type of evaluation, which Savin-Baden and Major define as follows:

1. A move away from traditional ideas of analysing data (such as codes and categories) by beginning with images and metaphors, which brings to the surface unconscious ideas and understandings, as well as helping to connect participants' experiences.
2. A recognition of the importance of the creative process in helping to facilitate the understanding of an issue by engaging with the whole person.
3. Values implicit in these kinds of evaluations becoming explicit, through the creative process which in turn enables the evaluator to shape the evaluation. The evaluation then connects with participants, as well as shaping the design throughout the life of the evaluation.
4. Data are both documented and represented through artistic expression. As a result the sense of peoples' experiences is realised through the creative process.

5. Interpretation is seen as an artistic process, so that the movement of different parts of data can be compared with a dance whereby the evaluator examines patterns, feelings and emotions of data in order to interpret them.
6. The concept of validity is broadened to incorporate understandings that emerge from artistic expression.
7. Dissemination of findings occurs through artistic forms. (Savin-Baden & Major, 2013: 281)

---

***Example***

Jaycox, L. H., McCaffrey, D. F., Ocampo, B.W., Shelley, G. A., Blake, S. M., Peterson, D. J., Richmond, L. S. and Kub, J. E. (2006) Challenges in the Evaluation and Implementation of School-Based Prevention and Intervention Programs on Sensitive Topics *American Journal of Evaluation* September 27 (3): 320-336,

The current emphasis on best practices for school-based health and mental health programs brings with it the demand for evaluation efforts in schools. This article describes the challenges of launching a successful school program and evaluation, with lessons learned from three projects that focus on intimate partner violence. The authors discuss issues related to constraints on the research design in schools, the recruitment of schools and participants within schools, program and evaluation implementation issues, the iterative implementation-evaluation cycle, and the dissemination of programs and study findings. The authors emphasize the need for flexibility and cultural awareness during all stages of the process.

---

*Arts-related Collaborative Approaches*

Many collaborative approaches take their roots from participatory action research and the variety of approaches has led advocates of these approaches in many and varied directions. Collaborative approaches focus on collaborative working in order to bring about action and change, usually emanating from within a group of people or organisation. Thus it is people who initiate change, rather than the researchers. In general, collaborative inquiry involves significant personal development for researchers, as they reflect on their behaviour and actions, as well as ensuring that they encourage others involved in the research to reflect on their behaviour. Collaborative inquiry is an approach that sees research as part of everyday life and therefore all our actions are also areas of inquiry. Thus in arts-related approaches, collaboration occurs throughout the study; from the initial question to the creation and representation of the findings.

*Example*

Parr, H. (2007) Collaborative film-making as process, method and text in mental health research *Cultural Geographies* 14 (1) 114-138,

This paper explores how film-making can assist as part of the development of sensitive and participative methodologies appropriate to accessing the worlds of people with severe and enduring mental health problems. It discusses how the film-making process can also act as a text that holds valuable data about the impact of the arts on mental health, and facilitates a range of mutually beneficial outcomes for those collaborating across usual academic/community divides. This agenda contributes to a consideration of the role of the arts in participative social geographies of mental health, and critically expands recent discussions about uses of video and film in a visual discipline.

*Reflective Pause*

The approaches mentioned so far in this chapter generally demonstrate a good fit philosophically with arts-related research. However, although researchers also do use the approaches set out below, these tend to be more post-positivist in their stance. This is because pragmatic qualitative research, phenomenology and grounded theory tend to be less collaborative than the approaches mentioned above, and thus tend to introduce a more bounded stance to arts-related research.

*Arts-related Pragmatic Qualitative Research*

Pragmatic qualitative research draws upon the most practical methods and often the easiest methods that will answer the chosen research question. Thus arts-related pragmatic qualitative research aims for a description of an experience or event as interpreted by the researcher. Researchers may take up arts-related pragmatic qualitative research when they want to provide a descriptive account from an interpretive perspective, and believe that no other research approach will suffice. Thus pragmatic qualitative research should be adopted when a researcher desires an eclectic and unique approach to understanding a phenomenon or event, as exemplified below:

*Example*

Tett, L., Anderson, K., McNeill, F., Overy, K and Sparks, R. (2012) Learning, Rehabilitation and the Arts in prisons: A Scottish Case *Study Studies in the Education of Adults* 44 (2) 171-185

*Continued*

135

This article investigates the role of the arts in enabling prisoners to engage with learning and improve their literacy, and the impact this has on their rehabilitation and desistance from crime. It draws on data collected from prisoners who participated in arts interventions in three different Scottish prisons. It argues that participating in the arts projects built an active learning culture and encouraged the improvement of verbal and written literacy skills through the use of positive pedagogical approaches. In addition participants learned to work together more effectively, developed self-confidence and were more trusting and supportive because they were working together on intensive projects that they had co-devised. For many prisoners, participation in the arts projects constructively challenged and disrupted the negative identities that they had internalised. Their public successes in performances before audiences of significant others opened up new personal and social identities (as artists or performers) that helped them to begin to envision an alternative self that in turn motivated them towards future desistance from crime.

*Arts-related Phenomenology*

Arts-related phenomenology is based on Heidegger's (rather than Husserl's) conceptualization of phenomenology, where the focus is on shedding light on taken for granted experiences that then enable researchers to create meaning and develop understanding. Heidegger focused on the hermeneutic circle, where the researcher moves from understanding the particular to having a sense of the whole, and then returns to the particular within an iterative cycle, which aims at developing a deeper understanding of the phenomena being studied. The difficulty with the use of phenomenology in arts-related research is that the researcher is expected to stand outside the situation and look in. This bracketing stands counter to much arts-related research, although phenomenology is still used, as exemplified below:

**Example**

Kirova, K and Emme, M. J. (2006) Using Photography as a means of Phenomenological Seeing: 'Doing Phenomenology' with Immigrant Children *Indo-Pacific Journal of Phenomenology*, 6(1). http://www.ipjp.org/SEmethod/ Special_Edition_Method-01_Kirova_&_Emme.pdf

The aim of the study presented in this paper was to understand the lifeworlds of children who experience immigration and whose lives are marked by dramatic changes in their being-in-the-world. More specifically, the study proceeded from the question: What does it mean for an immigrant child to enter school in a new country? Two methodological questions were also explored, namely (1) How

*Continued*

does one conduct a phenomenological investigation of a childhood phenomenon when the researchers and the participants do not share a common language? and (2) How does one engage children in the research process so that they provide not only 'thick' descriptions of their experiences using alternative, non-linguistic means, but also make meaning of these experiences?

In the current study, still photography was used to help the immigrant children recall and make meaning of what they experienced on their first day of school in a new country. In the process, they were enabled to become conscious photographers who came to see the world in such a way that photographic seeing became phenomenological seeing. Two examples of the children's visual narratives in the form of fotonovelas are presented to illustrate a methodology that involves fusion of the horizons surrounding the children, captured images of situations they encountered as they entered the classroom, and how the viewer saw the created image. The expanded notion of text and the use of digital technology in developing the text opened a space not only for visual representation of the children's lived experiences, but also for phenomenological analysis of these experiences. It is suggested that, although the written and visual texts produced as a result of the study differ, they are similar in the way in which they allow for phenomenological reflection and in their ability to show the phenomenon so as to evoke the reader's 'phenomenological nod'.

## Arts-related Grounded Theory

The origins of this theory tend to be located in relation to pragmatism and symbolic interactionism, and it is seen by many as a research approach that seeks to develop theory from data through constant comparison. There have been many arguments as to if it is indeed a research approach, or whether it is in fact just a means of managing and theorising about data collected. Glaser and Strauss (1967) formally developed the grounded theory approach, and suggested that when participants in a study each report many incidents, and create a total set of several hundred incidents, that then researchers can develop a theory from these. Thus rather than using a philosophical position or theoretical or conceptual framework, grounded theory research strives to develop a hypothesis directly from the data. However, as a result of this, most types of grounded theory today do not sit well with arts-related research, since grounded theory is formulaic, and this goes against creative interpretation that we believe is critical to arts-related research. The approach suggested by Charmaz (2006), of taking a constructivist orientation to grounded theory analysis, in which researchers and participants construct their own realities, is perhaps the only one that could work well with arts-related inquiry. This is because the researcher must acknowledge that their own interpretations of the phenomenon of study are in themselves constructions. Sutherland provides the following example of arts-related grounded theory:

137

---

*Example*

Sutherland, I. (2013). Arts-based methods in leadership development: Affording aesthetic workspaces, reflexivity and memory with momentum. *Management Learning*, 44(1), 25-43.

There is a growing cry for ways of approaching management and leadership development that embrace the complex, dynamic, chaotic and highly subjective, interactional environments of contemporary organisational contexts. One response has been the use of arts-based methods for management and leadership education. Although a community of research has grown around these practices, there remains a lack of empirically grounded work focusing on the underlying, situated, experiential learning processes of such methods. Working from the concept of experiential learning as knowledge creation through the transformation of experience, I develop a three-stage theoretical model that explores experiential learning processes of arts-based methodologies. This study is based on an inductive, grounded theory approach in analyzing descriptive essays written by Executive MBA students on their experiences of a choral conducting masterclass. The model describes how arts-based learning environments afford *aesthetic workspaces* where participants engaged *inaesthetic reflexivity* to create *memories with momentum* to inform their future leadership practice. This model builds an interdisciplinary bridge to the theory of affordances and the concepts of aesthetic workspaces and aesthetic reflexivity found within cultural sociology, a discourse with a focus on the reflexive use of the arts for self-configuration, regulation and development.

---

*Reflective Pause*

Thus we suggest that what is currently missing in most arts-related research is a consideration of how the research processes and artistic activities shape and are shaped by the researcher's and artist's stances politically, ontologically and semiotically. Perhaps to argue for a performative paradigm begins with the wrong question. Rather than asking whether we need a performative paradigm perhaps we should be asking what should we be cultivating? Stances and dispositions are more than knowledge and skills. Thus how do we cultivate a disposition for arts-related research? Furthermore, research, writing and presentation are not acultural or apolitical and are clearly located in understandings of identity and the way in which language, concepts and symbols are integrated by the individual, as Stogner reflects:

---

*Author Reflection*
*Two Sides of the Same Stone*
**Maggie Burnette Stogner**, Associate Professor, Film and Media Arts, American University, Washington D.C.

*The art form of the 21st century is video,* declared a Smithsonian Museum curator a couple of years ago. That statement already seems passé. Today's digital and internet technologies have given rise to new types of cultural expression far beyond the simple notion of moving images, from immersive multi-modal to mobile interactive and augmented virtual reality. Our discussions are filled with references to the latest Apps, new social media sites, cool tools such as Google Glasses, and trends in 3D and 4K. As we struggle to define these recent forms, much of the taxonomy remains rooted in the technological. It is time to turn our interpretative light on its enduring effect on our cultural content and context.

*The medium is the message,* declared Marshall McLuhan (1964) some fifty years ago. But today, the medium is the Instant Message. People share their thoughts, photos and videos instantly, around the world. They express themselves and respond immediately to the opinions of others. For the first time in history, we are creating a collective human story that transcends time and place. Often, there is no designated storyteller, no expert, no curator, not even a moderator. This highly anarchistic, often fragmented and random participation is unprecedented. What does it mean in terms of human reaction and interaction? Representation and authenticity? Ethics and best practices? What happens to the voices of those silenced by economic hardship or lack of freedom of expression?

*Plot is the basic principle,* declared the Greek philosopher Aristotle, some 2,300 years ago. His writings largely defined the ubiquitous classic, linear narrative that permeated our modern society until this millennium. In my research, I look at the ways in which cultural expression is shifting from expert-centric to user-centric, from local to global, from passive to participatory, from on-site to off-site, from linear to non-chronological, from real-time to asynchronous, and so on. These perimeters provide a new framework for understanding how we are creating, capturing and sharing today's cultural story.

As our tools of expression and creativity evolve, we need to expand our interpretative imaginations to harness deeper, lasting trends. In the throes of change, the differences between rock art and cyber graffiti might seem vast, but are they really?

What we are suggesting then is that instead of a new performative paradigm is a re-location of arts-related research as delineated in Table 9.2.

*Table 9.2. Re-location of arts-related research*

| Methodology | Philosophical stance | Key characteristics | Focus | Disciplinary origin |
|---|---|---|---|---|
| Arts-related narrative approaches | Constructivist Constructionist | Sharing and reflecting on situations and issues through stories | Development of a dialogic and collaborative story | Humanities (history and sociology) |
| Arts-related case study | Critical theory Constructivist Constructionist | Seeking to provide a real appraisal of everyday life of a given cultural group Analysing and interpreting the unit of study socioculturally | To understand and describe the everyday life of cultural groups | Education |
| Arts-related action research | Critical theory Constructivist Constructionist | Understanding and exploring power and control, while ensuring change for the better | Sharing of personal constructions to reach shared understanding and action | Psychology Education |
| Arts-related ethnography | Constructivist Constructionist | Collecting data through interviews, observation, writing and performing and representing data in critical ways | Use of dramatic art form to research and represent an exploration of the human condition | Anthropology |
| Arts-related evaluation | Constructivist Constructionist | Adopting the creative process to facilitate understanding of an issue by engaging with the whole person | Using art to portray the outcomes of evaluation | Education |
| Arts-related collaborative approaches | Constructivist Constructionist | Undertaking research in everyday life through reflecting on action Understanding how people see a particular action in everyday life | To understand and transform practices in order to understand and improve them | Psychology Education |
| Arts-related pragmatic qualitative research | Pragmatic | Practical and often related to practice Description of the data organised in a way that 'fits' | To adopt the most pragmatic option whatever the context | Professional fields |
| Arts-related phenomenology | Phenomenology | Understanding phenomena Interpreting data using self-reflection | To understand the meaning of being human in the world | Philosophy |
| Arts-related grounded theory | Pragmatic | Adoption of grounded theory methods but allowance for the notion that individuals construct their own realities. | Generation of theory with participant data as central | Sociology |

## CONCLUSION

Research paradigms and methodologies within arts-related research do not always sit easily with one another, with the result that collision and uncertainty can result in disquietude and a sense of fragmentation for those involved. We suggest that unease emerges from a lack both of familiarity with underlying philosophies that might underpin arts-related research, and of faith that such philosophies may indeed have something to offer to this relatively new field. However, we propose that what is important is to adopt paradigms, methodologies and stances that locate and support arts-related research, rather than to attempt to create naïve, realist solutions that muddy the waters rather than clarify them.

# CONCLUSION

Arts-related research remains a complex landscape of often troublesome ideals and practices. In many ways the challenges researchers face are bound up with issues of identity as much as the practical and philosophical choices they make. Thus although we have provided frameworks, models and suggestions for implementation we also acknowledge that arts-related research prompts us to deconstruct assumptions and live with the liminal.

Liminality was first coined by Arnold van Gennep and developed in his book The Rites of Passage in 1909. The term describes a psychological or metaphysical subjective state of being at the threshold of two existential planes, and although the term was originally applied to rites and rituals in small human groups, it was extended to whole societies by writers such as Jaspers (1953). Liminality also describes a sense of in-betweenness. Some forms of liminality appear to be more acceptable than others, since some are socially sanctioned, and others seek to maintain the status quo. However, much of the work on liminality to date has been based on rituals and rites of passage, whether becoming a man, a priest or a cancer patient. Perhaps arts-related research itself could be said to be liminal, since it sits in betwixt and between spaces methodologically and through it we are challenged to engage in identity work – the business of understanding how personal agency relates to the broader structures, historical circumstances and philosophical paradigms in which people live, work and learn.

Our journey through this text has challenged us to engage with the research assumptions that are and have been embedded in our shifting and changing identities. It has been a liminal journey that has prompted us to consider assumptions about our pedagogical, cultural and discipline-based stances. There have been times when we have questioned our involvement in arts-related research, wondering if we should really be artists; there have been other times when we have queried whether our strong view that paradigmatic and methodological positioning is important has been valid. The result is that liminality has brought a constant sense of disquietude, serving to confirm that identity work is not only an on-going task, but also a form of musical chairs:

> No 'beds 'are furnished for 're-embedding', and such beds as might be postulated and pursued prove fragile and often vanish before the work of 're-embedding' is complete. There are 'musical chairs', of various sizes and styles as well as of changing numbers and position, which prompt men and women to be constantly on the move and promise no 'fufillment', no rest and no satisfaction of 'arriving', of reaching the final destination, where one can disarm, relax and stop worrying. (Bauman, 2000:33–4)

For us arts-related research does have a real sense of shifting and changing, of possessing musical chairs. Yet this brings with it constant challenge and a recognition that often we have to examine our assumptions. Further, there is a need to acknowledge that the merging and emerging issues in our lives and work prompt us to ask difficult questions, such as:

> What happens to cultural narratives that are not technology-driven? How do we prevent homogenization? Is the authorial control inclusive? How can we ensure meaningful opportunities are available to all? In the Digital-Internet Age, story content and media represent the cultural artefacts of our century. By necessity, the role of storyteller and curator is merging. We are becoming an amalgamation, simultaneously telling and interpreting both personal and universal stories. The public's participation in creating and interpreting our cultural narrative is unprecedented. The shift is a significant one. And so is the responsibility. (Stogner, 2013)

It is our hope that this text has been a helpful exploration of ideas, case study examples, and reflective contributions from arts-related researchers in the field. Above all, we hope that it has been engaging, inspiring and most of all, useful. We hope too that we have stimulated ideas, sparked off new conversations and raised more questions which we encourage you to share with colleagues – and us as well. Through this text we have sought to find meaningful ways of disentangling what some artists might argue should not be disentangled when thinking about creativity and artistic endeavour. However, our ideas reflect our scholarly curiosity, and our excitement and respect for how the arts can contribute a rich and powerful aesthetic response to enliven our understanding of the world. Further, as Siegesmund and Cahnmann-Taylor (2008:242) have argued, arts-related research has a role in structured inquiry, not only to add to the palette of existing methodologies, but to push the boundaries of what research can illuminate and explore.

Thus we argue at the end of this text that arts-related research is not merely about the application of a variety of creative methods; instead it is the crafting of aesthetic expressions that disrupt and make the creative strange.

# NOTES ON CONTRIBUTORS

**Lynn Butler-Kisber** is a Professor of Education at McGill University in Montreal, and the Director of the office of Leadership in Community and International Initiatives, and of the Graduate Certificate in Educational Leadership Programs. She is the founding and current editor of The journal LEARNing Landscapes. Her research interests include qualitative and arts-based inquiry, leadership, literacy, and professional development, all grounded in socially just practices.

**Sue Challis** is a video artist whose work has been shown in the UK and internationally. In 2007 she was nominated for the Max Mara Art Prize for Women for her film 'Reading Agatha Christie'. She has BAs in Sociology and Fine Art, and MAs in Communication Management and Fine Art. For the past ten years she has worked as a participatory community artist, developing and delivering projects in London and the West Midlands. Sue is currently researching evaluation of the qualitative impact of creativity on participants in small and medium sized community projects in the West Midlands for Coventry University (Department of Geography, Environment and Disaster Management) and the ESRC. She is also consultant evaluator to several creative projects, including three pilots of an evaluation strategy for Arts Connect West Midlands, funded by the Arts Council.

**Alexandra Cutcher** is an award-winning academic in the School of Education at Southern Cross University (SCU), Australia. She believes in the power of the Arts to transform, educate, inspire and soothe. To this end, the provision of high quality Visual Arts education for students of all ages is a professional priority. Dr Cutcher's research interests focus on what the Arts can be and do; educationally, expressively, as research method, as language, as catharsis, as reflective instrument and as documented form. These understandings inform Alexandra's research agenda, her teaching and her spirited advocacy for Arts education.

**Robyn Ewing** is Professor of Teacher Education and the Arts at the University of Sydney. She teaches in the areas of curriculum, English and drama, working with both preservice and postgraduate teachers. Robyn is passionate about the Arts and education and the role quality arts experiences and processes can and should play across the curriculum and in educational research.

**Susan Finley** is Professor of Education at Washington State University Vancouver is the Founding Director of AHAS, a curriculum design based on the concepts of empowerment and democratic education and utilizes hands-on and arts-integrated learning approaches in all of its programs. The AHAS umbrella of programs began in 2002 with the AHAS Summer Program and the project to offer tutoring in shelters. Teachers in AHAS programs are guided by the educational theories of critical pedagogy conceptualized in the works of Paulo Freire. Finley has been guest editor of several journals devoted to arts-based research, including Qualitative Inquiry, Cultural Studies-Critical Methodologies, and International Journal of Qualitative Studies in Education. She has also contributed to several research handbooks including the Sage Handbook of Arts in Education and the Sage Handbook of Qualitative Research.

**Spencer J. Harrison,** is an artist, a human rights activist, a storyteller, and an educator. He combines all aspects of this identity into what he calls "his studio practice." He presently teaches in the Faculty of Art, in Drawing and Painting at OCAD University, Toronto, Canada. The focus of his courses are not the instruction of how to paint, but rather "why paint?" and "why are you the one doing that painting?" His education includes; a BFA from Queen's University, Kingston, Ontario; a Master's in Canadian Heritage and Development Studies from Trent University, Peterborough, On; and a Doctorate in Adult Education and Community Development from the Ontario Institute for Studies in Education of the University of Toronto, Toronto, Ontario. His PhD is noted as the first painted dissertation in Canada.

**Carl Leggo** is a poet and professor at the University of British Columbia. His books include: Growing Up Perpendicular on the Side of a Hill; View from My Mother's House; Come-By-Chance; Teaching to Wonder: Responding to Poetry in the Secondary Classroom; and Sailing in a Concrete Boat: A Teacher's Journey.

**Maks Del Mar** is Senior Lecturer in Law and Philosophy and Director of the Centre for Law and Society in a Global Context (CLSGC) in the Department of Law, Queen Mary University of London. He is also Academic Fellow of the Honourable Society of the Inner Temple. He completed a BA in Philosophy and Literature with First Class Honours and a LLB with First Class Honours at the University of Queensland, Australia. He then served as an Associate to the Hon. Justice Margaret White at the Supreme Court of Queensland, before qualifying and practising as a solicitor. He has completed two doctorates: one in Law from the University of Edinburgh, and one in the Social Sciences from the University of Lausanne. He has a long-standing interest in the pedagogical potential of the arts in law schools, stemming from his involvement in the AHRC Beyond Text in Legal Education Network at the University of Edinburgh (2007-8). Together with Paul Maharg and Zenon Bankowski, he is the co-editor of *The Arts and the Legal Academy* (Ashgate, 2013).

**Elelwani Ramugondo** is Associate Professor within the Division of Occupational Therapy, University of Cape Town. Regarded as a play-activist, Elelwani draws from research and everyday observations on children's play and the arts to explain the politics of human occupation within the context of rapid social change, and to raise occupational consciousness. Her own research takes an intergenerational approach, and negates the adult-child binary often prevalent within the study of play and the arts.

**Maggie Burnette Stogner** is an Associate Professor of film and media arts at American University's School of Communication in Washington D.C. She is founder of Blue Bear Films, a global media design and production company of documentaries and immersive media. Her creative work includes the award-winning, world-touring exhibitions: Roads of Arabia; Tutankhamun and the Golden Pharaohs; Real Pirates; Afghanistan: Hidden Treasures; and Indiana Jones and the Adventure of Archaeology with Harrison Ford. From 1995 to 2005, Maggie was a producer and then Senior Producer of National Geographic's weekly award-winning documentary program Explorer. Her graduate degree in documentary film is from Stanford University.

**Marcus Weaver-Hightower** is Associate Professor and chair of Educational Foundations and Research, University of North Dakota. His research focuses on boys and masculinity, food politics, the politics and sociology of education and policy, comics and graphic novels, and qualitative methods. He the author of *The Politics of Policy in Boys' Education: Getting Boys "Right"* and other articles and collections.

# REFERENCES

Adelman, C., Jenkins, D., & Kemmis, S. (1980). Rethinking case study: Notes from the second Cambridge conference. In H. Simons (Ed.), *Towards a science of the singular* (pp. 45–61). Norwich: Centre for Applied Research in Education, University of East Anglia.

Aldridge, D. (1989). Music, communication and medicine. *Royal Society of Medicine, 8*(2), 743–746.

Aldridge, D. (1990). Meaning and expression: The pursuit of aesthetics in research. *Holistic Medicine, 5*, 177–186.

Aldridge, A. (2008). Therapeutic narrative analysis: A methodological proposal for the interpretation of musical traces, In P. Liamputtong & J. Rumbold (Eds.), *Knowing differently: Arts-based research and collaborative research* (pp. 205–227). New York, NY: Nova Science Publishers.

Alexander, H. (2003). Aesthetic inquiry in education: Community, transcendence and the meaning of pedagogy. *Journal of Aesthetic Education, 37*(2), 1–17.

Al-Jawad, M. (2013). Comics are research: Graphic narratives as a new way of seeing clinical practice. *Journal of Medical Humanities.* doi: 10.1007/s10912-013-9205

Apol, L. (2013, April–May). *The challenge and responsibility of researcher as writer and witness: Poetry from Rwanda.* Paper presented at AERA Annual Meeting and Exhibition, San Francisco, CA.

Aristotle, G. F. (1967). (G. F. Else, Trans.). *Poetics* (p. 28). Michigan, MI: University of Michigan Press.

Armitage, L., & Welsby, J. (2009). Communicating arts-based inquiry: There are no flesh tones in black or white. In J. Higgs, D. Horsfall, & S. Grace (Eds.), *Writing qualitative research on practice* (pp. 105–114). Rotterdam: Sense Publishers.

Arora, R. (2013). *Discovering the postmodern nomad: A metaphor for an artful inquiry into the career stories of emerging adults transitioning under the Caribbean sun* (Unpublished doctoral dissertation). McGill University, Montreal, QC.

Arts Council England. (2007). *The arts, health and well-being.* London: Arts Council England.

Arts Council England/Department of Health. (2007). *A prospectus for arts and health.* London: Arts Council England/Department of Health.

Ayers, W., & Alexander-Tanner, R. (2010). *To teach: The journey, in comics.* New York, NY: Teachers College Press.

Bamford, A. (2005, February). *The art of research: Digital theses in the arts.* Retrieved February 17, 2006 from http://adt.caul.edu.au/edt2005/papers/123Bamford.pdf

Banks, M. (2000). Visual anthropology: Image, object and interpretation. In J. Posser (Ed.), *Image-based research. A sourcebook for qualitative researchers* (pp. 9–23). London: Routledge Falmer.

Barbican press release. (2013, March). Retrieved June 06, 2014 from https://www.barbican.org.uk/news/artformnews/art/visual-art-2012-random-internati

Barnes, J. (2013). Drama to promote social and personal well-being in six and seven year olds with communication difficulties: The speech bubbles project, *Perspectives in Public Health.* Retrieved July 7, 2014, from http://create.canterbury.ac.uk/12291/

Barnett, R. (1994). *The limits of competence.* Buckingham: Open University Press/SRHE.

Barnett, R. (1997). *Higher education: A critical business.* Buckingham: Open University Press/SRHE.

Barrett, E., & Bolt, B. (2007). *Practice as research approaches to creative arts enquiry.* London: IB Tauris.

Barrett, E. (2007). Foucaults what is an author: Towards a critical discourse of practice as research. In E. Barrett & B. Bolt (Eds.), *Practice as research: Approaches* (pp. 135–146). London, England: IB Tauris London.

Barone, T. (1983). Things of use and things of beauty: The story of the Swain County High School Arts Program. *Daedalus, 112*(3), 1–28.

Barone, T. (1989). Ways of being at risk: The case of Billy Charles Barnett. *Phi Delta Kappan, 71*, 147–151.

Barone, T. (2000). *Aesthetics, politics, and educational theory: Essay and examples.* New York, NY: Peter Lang.

# REFERENCES

Barone, T. (2001). *Touching eternity: The enduring outcomes of teaching.* New York, NY: Teachers College Press.

Barone, T., & Eisner, E. (1997). Arts-based educational research. In R. M. Jaeger (Ed.), *Complementary methods for research in education* (2nd ed., pp. 75–116). Washington, DC: American Educational Research Association.

Barone, T., & Eisner, E. (2006). Arts-based educational research. In J. Green, G. Camilli, & P. Elmore (Eds.), *Complementary methods in research in education* (pp. 95–109). Mahwah, NJ: Lawrence Erlbaum Associates.

Barone, T., & Eisner, E. W. (1997). Arts-based educational research. In R. M. Jaeger (Ed.), *Complementary methods for research in education* (pp. 73–98). Washington, DC: AERA.

Barone, T., & Eisner, E. W. (2012). *Arts based research.* London: Sage.

Batt-Rawden, K. B., & Tellnes, G. (2005). Nature-culture-health activities as a method of rehabilitation: An evaluation of participants' health, quality of life and function. *International Journal of Rehabilitation Research, 28,* 175–180.

Bauman, Z. (2000). *Liquid modernity.* Cambridge: Polity Press

Beck, J. L., Belliveau, G., Lea, G. W., & Wager, A. (2011). Delineating a spectrum of research-based theatre. *Qualitative Inquiry, 17*(8), 687–700.

Behar, R. (2007). *Ethnography in a time of blurred genres essay.* Retrieved June 11, 2014 from http:// deepblue.lib.umich.edu/bitstream/handle/2027.42/74973/ahu.2007.32.2.145.pdf?sequence=1

Behar, R. (2003). Ethnography and the book that was lost. *Ethnography, 4*(1), 15–39.

Behar, R. (1996). *The vulnerable observer: Anthropology that breaks your heart.* Boston, MA, Beacon Press.

Belardinelli, R., Lacalaprice, F., Ventrella, C., Volpe, L., & Faccenda, E. (2008). Waltz dancing in patients with chronic heart failure: New forms of exercise training. *Heart Failure, 1*(2), 107–114.

Benetar, S. R. (2002). The HIV/AIDS pandemic: A sign of instability in a complex global system. *The Journal of Medicine & Philosophy, 27*(2), 163–177.

Bennett, D., Wright, D., & Blom, D. (2010). The Artistic practice-Research-Teaching (ART) Nexus: Translating the information flow. *Journal of University Teaching & Learning Practice, 7*(2). Retrieved June 10, 2014 from http://ro.uow.edu.au/jutlp/vol7/iss2/3

Bequette, J., & Bequette, M. B. (2012). A place for art and design education in the STEM conversation. *Art Education, 65*(92), 40–47.

Berger, A. A. (1998). *Signs in contemporary culture: An introduction to semiotics.* Salem, WI: Sheffield Publishers Co.

Blom, D. (2006). Preparing Ross Edwards's Kumari for performance: Conceptual planning. In S. Macarthur, B. Crossman, & R. Morelos (Eds.), *Intercultural music: Creation and interpretation* (pp. 111–115). Sydney: Australian Music Centre.

Blumenfeld-Jones, D. (1995). Dance as a mode of research representation. *Qualitative Inquiry, 1*(4), 391–401.

Boal, A. (1979). *Theatre of the oppressed.* London: Pluto Press.

Bolt, B. (2004). *Art beyond representation: The performative power of the image.* London and New York: I.B. Tauris.

Bolt, B. (2006, June). A non standard deviation: Handlability, praxical knowledge and practice led research. Paper delivered at the conference *Speculation and Innovation: Applying practice led research in the Creative Industries.* Retrieved June 8, 2009 from http://artsresearch.brighton.ac.uk/ links/practiceled/Bolt2005.pdf

Bolt, B. (2007). The magic in is handling. In E. Barrett & B. Bolt (Eds.), *Practice as research: Approaches to creative arts enquiry* (pp. 27–34). London, England: I.B. Tauris.

Bourriaud, N. (2002). *Relational aesthetics,* Translated by Simon Pleasance & Fronza Woods. Dijon-Quetigny, France: Les presses du réel (p.13). Retrieved July 11, 2014 from http://isites.harvard.edu/ fs/docs/icb.topic641765.files/6%20b%20Bourriaud_Relational%20Aesthetics_Foreward%20and%20 Relational%20Form.pdf

Boydell, K. M. (2011). Making sense of collective events: The co-creation of a research based dance [43 paragraphs]. *Forum Qualitative Sozialforschung/Forum: Qualitative Social Research, 12*(1), Art. 5. Retrieved July 11, 2014 from http://nbn-resolving.de/urn:nbn:de:0114-fqs110155

Boyle, D. (2011). *Exploring a university teacher's approach to incorporating music in a cognition course* (Unpublished PhD dissertation). McGill University, Montreal, QC.

Bruner, J. (1986). *Actual minds, possible worlds*. Cambridge, MA: Harvard University.

Bruner, J. (1990). *Acts of meaning*. Cambridge, MA: Harvard University Press.

Bruner, J. (1996). *The culture of education*. Cambridge, MA: Harvard University Press.

Bruns. A., & Schmidt, J. H. (2012). Produsage: A closer look at continuing developments. *New Review of Hypermedia and Multimedia, 17*(1), 3–8. Retrieved June 9, 2014 from http://eprints.qut.edu.au/48818/1/Produsage_Editorial.pdf

Brunker, N. (2012). *Conceptualising children's social and emotional wellbeing: portraits of lived meanings in primary schooling* (Unpublished PhD dissertation). Sydney: University of Sydney.

Bruns, A. (2008). *Blogs, wikipedia, second life, and beyond: From production to produsage*. New York, NY: Peter Lang.

Bullough, R. V., & Pinnegar, S. (2001). Guidelines for quality in autobiographical forms of self-study research. *Educational Researcher, 30*(3), 13–21.

Burgess, J. (2006). Hearing ordinary voices: Cultural studies, vernacular creativity and digital storytelling. *Continuum: Journal of Media & Cultural Studies 20*(2), 201–214.

Butler-Kisber, L. (2010). *Qualitative inquiry: Thematic, narrative and arts-informed perspectives*. London: Sage.

Butler-Kisber, L. (2008). Collage as inquiry. In J. G. Knowles & A. L. Cole (Eds.), *Handbook of education and the arts in qualitative research* (pp. 265–276). Thousand Oaks, CA: Sage.

Butler-Kisber, L. (2010). *Qualitative inquiry: Thematic, narrative and arts-informed perspectives*. London: Sage.

Butler-Kisber, L., & Poldama, T. (2010). The power of visual approaches in qualitative inquiry: The use of collage making and concept mapping in experiential research. *Journal of Research Practice, 6*(2), 1–12.

Cahnmann-Taylor M., & Siegesmund, R. (Eds.). (2008). *Arts-based research in education*. London: Routledge.

Campbell, V. (2013). *The Selkie Project* (Unpublished PhD dissertation). Sydney: University of Sydney.

Candy, L., & Edmonds, E. (2002). Interaction in art and technology crossings. *Electronic Journal of Art and Technology, 2*(1). Retrieved June 19, 2014 from http://crossings.tcd.ie/issues/2.1/Candy/

Cancienne, M. B. (2008). Dance as method: The process and product of movement in educational research. Vignette Two – Using improvisational dance to analyze a community walk project. In P. Liamputtong & J. Rumbold (Eds.), *Knowing differently: Arts-based and collaborative research* (pp. 169–186). New York, NY: Nova Science Publishers, Inc.

Cancienne, M. B., & Snowber, C. (2003). Writing rhythm: Movement as method. *Qualitative Inquiry, 9*(2), 237–253.

Carson, T., & Sumara, D. (1997). *Action research as a living practice*. New York, NY: Peter Lang.

Catterall, J. S., Chapleau, R., & Iwanaga, J. (1999). Involvement in the arts and human development. In E. B. Fiske (Ed.), *Champions of change: The impact of the arts on learning* (pp. 1–18). Washington, DC: Arts Education Partnership.

Carey, J. (2005). *What good are the arts?* London: Faber & Faber.

Chafer, J., with the Avatar Repertory Theater. (2010). *Alice in wonderland*. Second Life. Retrieved July 8, 2014 from http://ireport.cnn.com/docs/DOC-436692

Challis, S. (2013). Sketchbook postal exchange. *Journal of Writing in Creative Practice, 6*(2), 187–211.

Challis, S. (2014). *Maximising impact: Connecting creativity, participation and impact in the qualitative evaluation of creative community project*. (Unpublished PhD dissertation). Coventry, UK: Coventry University, Department of Geography, Environment and Disaster Management.

Challis, S. (2013). *Artist-Evaluators: How creativity itself can challenge the limitations of qualitative evaluation in creative community projects: Evidence from the UK West Midlands*. The European Conference on Arts and Humanities Brighton, UK 2013, Conference Proceedings, pp. 265–278.

Chang, H. (2008). *Autoethnography as method*. Walnut Creek, CA: Left Coast Press.

Charmaz, K. (2006). *Constructing grounded theory: A practical guide through qualitative analysis*. London: Sage.

# REFERENCES

Clandinin, D. J., & Connolly, M. (2000). *Narrative inquiry: Experience and story in qualitative research.* San Francisco, CA: Jossey-Bass.

Clift, S., Camic, P., Chapman, B., Clayton, G., Daykin, N., Eades, G., ... White, M. (2009). The state of arts and health in England. *Arts and Health, 9*(1), 6–35.

Clift, S. (Ed.). (2006). Recent developments in the arts and health field in the UK. *Journal of the Royal Society for the Promotion of Health, Special Issue on Arts Health, 3,*109.

Clift, S., & Vella-Burrows, T. (2003). *Arts and healthy communities in the South East.* Report for the Arts Council England, South East Canterbury: Canterbury Christ Church University College.

Cole, A. L., & Knowles, J. G. (2008). Arts-informed research. In J. G. Knowles & A. L. Cole (Eds.), *Handbook of education and the arts in qualitative research.* Thousand Oaks, CA: Sage, 55–70.

Coleridge, S. T. (1817). *Biographia literaria.* New Jersey, NJ: Princeton University Press (Printed 1983).

Conquergood, D. (2002). Performance studies: Interventions and radical research. *Drama Review: A Journal of Performative Studies, 46,* 145–156.

Conrad, D., & Campbell, G. (2008). Participatory Research – An empowering methodology with marginalized populations. In P. Liamputtong & J. Rumbold (Eds.), *Knowing Differently: Arts-based and collaborative research* (pp. 247–263). New York, NY: Nova Science Publishers.

Conroy, J. (2004). *Betwixt and between: The liminal imagination, education and democracy.* New York, NY: Peter Lang.

Cooper, A. (2001). Beyond the icon: The role of the image in human computer interface (HCI) design. *Digital Creativity, 12*(2), 99–102

Cornock, S., & Edmonds, E. (1973). The creative process where the artist is amplified or superseded by the computer. *Leonardo, 6,* 11–16.

Cotterill, P., & Letherby, G. (1994). The person in the researcher. In R. Burgess (Ed.), *Studies in qualitative methodology* (pp. 107–136). London: Jai press.

Cousin, G. (2009). *Researching learning in higher education: An introduction to contemporary methods and approaches.* New York and Abingdon: Routledge.

Crossman, B. (2006). Moving between things: Heaven and hell, visual and sonic gestures towards transcendent oneness. In S. Macarthur, B. Crossman, & R. Morelos (Eds.), *Intercultural music: Creation and interpretation* (pp. 45–50). Sydney: Australian Music Centre.

Crotty, M. (1988). *The foundations of social research: Meaning and perspective in the research process.* London, Thousand Oaks, CA, and New Delhi: SAGE Publications.

Csikszentmihalyi, M. (1996). *Creativity: Flow and the psychology of discovery and invention.* New York, NY: Harper Perennial.

Csikszentmihaly, M. (2002). *Flow.* London: Random House.

Czarniawska, B. (2004). *Narratives in social science research.* London: Sage.

Davis, D., & Butler-Kisber, L. (1999, April). Arts-based representation in qualitative research: Collage as a contextualizing strategy. Paper presented at the Annual Meeting of the American Educational Research Association. Montreal, QC.

Daykin, N. (2008). Knowing through music: Implications for research. In P. Liamputtong & J. Rumbold (Eds.), *Knowing differently: Arts-based and collaborative research method* (pp. 229–243). New York, NY: Nova Science Publishers, Inc.

Delbecq, A. L., & Vandeven, A. H. (1971). A group process model for problem identification and program planning. *Journal Of Applied Behavioral Science, VII,* 466–491.

Department of Health, Arts Council England. (2007). A prospectus for arts and health. Retrieved March 8, 2012 from http://www.artscouncil.org.uk/publication_archive/a-prospectus-for-arts-and-health/

DeMoss, K., & Morris, T. (2002). *How arts integration supports student learning: Students shed light on the connections. Arts Integration and learning.* Chicago, IL: Chicago Arts Partnerships in Education (CAPE). Retrieved July 17, 2014 from http://www.artsedsearch.org/summaries/how-arts-integration-supports-student-learning-students-shed-light-on-the-connections

Denzin, N. (2003). *Performance ethnography: Critical pedagogy and the politics of culture.* Thousand Oaks, CA: Sage.

Denzin, N. K. (2000). Aesthetics and the practices of qualitative inquiry. *Qualitative Inquiry, 6*(2), 256-265.

Denzin, N. K. (1978). *The research act: A theoretical introduction to sociological methods.* New York, NY: McGraw Hill.

Denzin, N. K. (1997). *Interpretive ethnography: Ethnographic practices for the 21st century.* Thousand Oaks, CA: Sage.

Denzin, N. K. (2001). *Interpretive interactionism* (2nd ed). Newbury Park, CA: Sage.

Derrida, J. (1992). *The other heading: Reflections on today's Europe.* (P. A. Brault & M. P. Naas, Trans.). Bloomington and Indianapolis: Indiana University Press.

Dewey, J. (1931). *Philosophy and civilization.* New York, NY: Minton Balch.

Dewey, J. (1938). *Experience and education.* New York, NY: Collier Books.

Dewey, J. (1983). *Art as experience.* New York, NY: Perigee Books.

Diamond, C. P., & Mullen, C. A. (1999). *The postmodern educatory: Arts based inquiries and teacher development.* New York, NY: Peter Lang.

Diamond, C. T. P., & Mullen, C. A. (Eds.). (1999). *The postmodern educator: Arts based inquiries and teacher development.* New York, NY: Peter Lang.

Diamond, C.P., & Mullen, C.A. (2000). Rescripting the script and rewriting the paper: Taking research to the edge of the exploratory. *International Journal of Education and the Arts, 1*(4), 1–23.

Dickens, A. P., Richards, S. H., Greaves, C. J., & Campbell, J. L. (2011). Interventions targeting social isolation in older people: A systematic review. *BMC Public Health, 11*, 647.

Diversi, M. (2008). Young and strapped in America: Learning through short story about Latino youth finding meaning in Tupac's Rap. In P. Liamputtong & J. Rumbold (Eds.), *Knowing differently: Arts-based and collaborative research methods* (pp. 67–80). New York, NY: Nova Science Publishers.

Dose, L. (2006). National network for the arts in health: Lessons learned from six years of work. *Journal of the Royal Society for the Promotion of Health, 126*(3), 110–112.

Duncan, M. (2004). Women empowered through occupation: From deprivation to realized potential. In R. Watson & L. Swartz (Eds.), *Transformation through occupation* (pp. 103–118). Philadelphia, PA: Whurr Publishers.

Dunlop, R. (2000). *Boundary Bay: A novel as educational research* (Unpublished Doctoral dissertation). University of British Columbia, Vancouver, BC.

Edmonds, E. A., & Leggett, M. (2010). How artists fit into research processes. *Leonardo, 43*(2), 194–195.

Edmonds, E. A., Bilda, Z., & Muller, L. (2009). Artist, evaluator and curator: Three viewpoints on interactive art, evaluation and audience experience. *Digital Creativity, 20*, 141–151.

Eisner, E. (2006). Does arts-based research have a future? Inaugural lecture for the first European conference in arts-based research. *Studies in Art Education, 48*(1), 9–18.

Eisner, E. (1985). *The art of educational evaluation: A personal view.* London: Falmer Press.

Eisner, E. (1991). *The enlightened eye: Qualitative inquiry and the enhancement of educational practice.* New York, NY: Macmillan.

Eisner, E. (1998). *The enlightened eye: Qualitative inquiry and the enhancement of educational practice.* Upper Saddle River, NJ: Merrill.

Eisner, E. (2002). *An agenda for research in arts education: Arts and the creation of mind.* New Haven, CT: Yale University Press.

Eisner, E. (2009). Persistent tensions in arts based research. In M. Cahnmann-Taylor & R. Siegesmind (Eds.), *Arts based research in education* (pp. 22–27). London: Routledge.

Eisner, E. W. (1997). The promise and perils of alternative forms of data representation, *Educational Researcher, 26*(6), 4–10.

Eisner, E., & Peshkin, A. (1990). *Qualitative inquiry in education: The continuing debate.* New York, NY: Teachers College Press.

Elbaz, F. (1983). *Teacher thinking: A study of practical knowledge.* London: Croom Helm.

English, A., & Stengel, B. (2010). Exploring fear: Rousseau, Dewey, and Freire on fear and learning. *Educational Theory, 60*(5), 521–542.

Estrell, K., & Forinash, M. (2007). Perspectives narrative inquiry and arts-based inquiry: Multinarrative. *Journal of Humanistic Psychology, 47*(3), 376–383.

Ettinger, B. (2011). Art as compassion (Catherine de Zegher & Griselda Pollock, Trans.).

Ewing, R., & Hughes, J. (2008). Arts-Informed inquiry in teacher education: Contesting the myths. *European Educational Research Journal, 7*(4), 512–522.

Faltis, C. (2013). Eradicating borders: An exploration of scholartistry for embracing mexican immigrant children and youth in education. *Journal of Language and Literacy Education, 9*(2), 50–62.

REFERENCES

Fewster, R., Woods, D., & Chafer, J. (2010). Staging second life in real and virtual spaces. In G. Vincenti & J. Braman (Eds.), *Teaching through multi-user virtual environments: Applying dynamic elements to the modern classroom* (pp. 217–233). Hershey, PA: IGI Global.

Finley, S. (2000). Dream child. *Qualitative Inquiry, 6*(3), 432–434.

Finley, S. (2003). Arts-based inquiry in QI: Seven years from crisis to guerilla warfare. *Qualitative Inquiry, 9*(2), 281–296.

Finley, S. (2005). Arts-based inquiry: Performing revolutionary pedagogy. In N. K. Denzin & Y. S. Lincoln (Eds.), *The SAGE handbook of qualitative research* (3rd ed., pp. 681–694). Thousand Oaks, CA: Sage.

Finley, S. (2008). Arts-based research. In J. G. Knowles & A. L. Cole (Eds.), *Handbook of the arts in qualitative research* (pp. 71–82). London: Sage.

Foucault, M. (1979). *Discipline and punish: The birth of the prison.* Harmondsworth: Penguin Books.

Freire, P. (1970). *Pedagogy of the oppressed.* New York, NY: Continuum.

Frogett, L., Little, R., Roy, A., & Whitaker, L. (2011, October). *New model visual arts organisations & social engagement.* University of Central Lancashire, Psychosocial Research Unit, Lancashire.

Furlini, L. (2005). *Living with chronic dementia from the caregiver perspective: A case for educational support* (Unpublished doctoral dissertation). McGill University, Montreal, QC.

Gee, J.P. (n.d). The new literacy studies & the social turn. Retrieved June 14, 2014 from http://www.schools.ash.org.au/litweb/page300.html Accessed December 6, 2006.

Geertz, C. (1983). Blurred genres: The refiguration of social thought. *Local knowledge: Further essays in interpretive anthropology* (pp. 19–35). New York, NY: Basic Books.

Giddens, A. (1984). *The constitution of society.* Cambridge, UK: Policy Press.

Giddens, A., & Pierson, C. (1998). *Conversations with Anthony Giddens: Making sense of modernity.* Cambridge, UK: Polity Press.

Gilman, S. (1988). *Disease & representation: Images of illness from madness to AIDS.* New York, NY: Cornell University Press.

Glaser, B. G., & Strauss, A. L. (1967). *Discovery of grounded theory: Strategies for qualitative research.* New York, NY: Aldine De Gruyter.

Gordon, I. (2012, June). *Can digital storytelling enhance the employability of occupational therapy students?* Paper presented at the 36th annual conference of occupational therapy.

Graham, M., & Goetz Zwirn, S. (2010). How being a teaching artist can influence K-12 art education. *Studies in Art Education, 51*(3), 219–232.

Gray, R. E. (2003). Performing on & off the stage: The place(s) of performance in arts-based approaches to qualitative inquiry. *Qualitative Inquiry, 9*(2), 254–267.

Greaves C. J., & Farbus, L. (2006). Effects of creative & social activity on the health & well-being of socially isolated older people: Outcomes from a multi-method observational study. *The Journal of the Royal Society for the Promotion of Health, 126*(3), 134–142.

Green, M. J. (2013). Missed it. *Annals of Internal Medicine, 158*(5), 357–361.

Greenwood, J. (2012). Arts-based research: Weaving magic & meaning. *International Journal of Education & the Arts, 13*(1). Retrieved June 04, 2014 from http://www.ijea.org/v13i1/

Guba, E. G., & Lincoln, Y. S. (1994). Competing paradigms in qualitative research. In N. K. Denzin & Y. S. Lincoln (Eds.), *Handbook of qualitative research.* Thousand Oaks, CA: Sage.

Guba, E. G., & Lincoln, Y. S. (2005). Paradigmatic controversies, contradictions, and emerging confluences. In N. K. Denzin & Y. S. Lincoln (Eds.), *The SAGE handbook of qualitative research* (3rd ed). Thousand Oaks, CA: Sage.

Gupta, A. (2010). Rethinking aristotle's poetics: The pragmatic aspect of art & knowledge. *Journal of Aesthetic Education, 44*(4), 60–80.

Hatton, N., & Smith, D. (1995). Reflection in teacher education – towards definition and implementation. *Teaching and Teacher Education, 11*(1), 3–49.

Habron, J., Butterly, F., Gordon, I., & Roebuck, A. (2013). Being well, being musical: Music composition as a resource and occupation for older people. *British Journal of Occupational Therapy, 76*(7), 308–316.

Heath, S. B., & Roach, A. (1999). Imaginative actuality: Learning in the arts during non-school hours. In E. Fisk (Ed.), *Champions of change: The impact of the arts on learning* (pp. 19–34). Washington, DC: Arts Education Partnership and President's Committee on the Arts and the Humanities.

Heath, S. B., Soep, E., & Roach A. (1998). Living the arts through language-learning: A report on community-based youth organizations. *American for the Arts Monographs, 2*(7), 1–20.

Hecq, D., & Banagan, R. (2009). *Practice, research and their phantom limb* [Review of Hazel Smith & Roger T Dean, practice-led research, research-led practice in the creative arts]. Retrieved June 07, 2014 from http://www.textjournal.com.au/april10/hecq_banagan_rev.htm

Hacking, S., Secker, J., Kent, L., Shenton, J., & Spandler, H. (2006). Mental health and arts participation: The state of the art in England. *Journal of the Royal Society for the Promotion of Health, 126*, 121–127.

Hampshire, K. R., & Matthijsse, M. (2010). Can arts projects improve young people's wellbeing? A social capital approach. *Social Science Medicine, 71*(4), 708–716.

Hannan, M. (2006). Making music: Inside/outside. *RealTime, 74*, 6–8.

Hannemann, B. T. (2006). Creativity with dementia patients: Can creativity and art stimulate dementia patients positively? *Gerontology, 52*(1), 59–65.

Hannula, M. (2009). Catch me if you can: Chances and challenges of artistic research, art & research: A journal of ideas, contexts and methods, *2*(2). Retrieved July 09, 2014 from http://www.artandresearch.org.uk/v2n2/hannula1.html

Harrison, S.J. (2013, April). *Not a freak show: Growing up gay in rural Ontario in the 1960s without narratives, images or role models upon which to formulate an identity.* Paper presented at AERA Annual Meeting and Exhibition, San Francisco, CA.

Hasebe-Ludt, E., Chambers, C., Oberg, A., & Leggo, C. (2008a). Embracing the world, with all our relations: Métissage as an artful braiding. In S. Springgay, R. Irwin, C. Leggo, & P. Gouzouasis (Eds.), *Being with a/r/tography* (pp. 57–23). Rotterdam, NL: Sense Publishers.

Hasebe-Ludt, E., Chambers, C., Leggo, C., Hurren, W., Oberg, A., & Donald, D. (2008b). Métissage. In A. L. Cole & J. G. Knowles (Eds.), *Handbook of the arts in qualitative social science research* (pp. 141–153). Thousand Oaks, CA: Sage.

Hasebe-Ludt, E., Chambers, C., & Leggo, C. (2009). *Life writing and literary métissage as an ethos for our times.* New York, NY: Peter Lang.

Haseman, B. (2006). A manifesto for performative research. Media international Australia incorporating culture and policy, theme issue. *Practice-led Research, 118*, 98–106. Retrieved April 04, 2014 from http://eprints.qut.edu.au/3999/1/3999_1.pdf

Haseman, B. (2008). Rupture and recognition: Identifying the performative research paradigm. In E. Barrett & B. Bolt (Eds.), *Practice as research: Approaches to creative arts inquiry* (pp. 147–157). London and New York: I.B Tauris.

Haseman, B. C., & Mafe, D. J. (2009). Acquiring know-how: Research training for practice-led researchers. In H. Smith & R. T. Dean (Eds.), *Practice-led Research. Research-Led practice in the creative arts* (pp. 211–228). Edinburgh: Edinburgh University Press.

Health Development Agency. (2004). *Taking action: Improving the health and wellbeing of people in mid-life and beyond.* London: Health Development Agency.

Heenan, D. (2006). Art as therapy: An effective way of promoting positive mental health? *Disability and Society, 21*(2), 179–191.

Herman, L. (2005). Researching the images of evil events: An arts-based methodology in liminal space. *Qualitative Inquiry, 11*(3), 468–480.

Heidegger, M. (1927/1962). *Being and time.* New York, NY: Harper.

Hockney, D. (2008). *Drawing in a printing machine.* Retrieved July 15, 2014 from http://www.lalouver.com/resource/hockney_08/Hockney_09.pdf

Hockney, D. (2008). *Hockney on art: Conversations with Paul Joyce.* London, UK: Little Brown Company.

Hodson, L. (2012). The art of the possible: Relationships in teaching and learning (Unpublished PhD dissertation). University of Sydney, Sydney.

Hollway, W., & Jefferson, T. (2000). *Doing qualitative research differently.* London: Sage.

Holm, G. (2008). Photography as a performance. *Forum Qualitative Sozialforschung/Forum: Qualitative Social Research, 9*(2), Retrieved July 15, 2014 from http://nbn-resolving.de/urn:nbn:de:0114-fqs0802380

Hooks, b. (1994). *Teaching to transgress.* London: Routledge.

Howells, V., & Zelnik, T. (2009). Making art: A qualitative study of personal and group transformation in a community arts studio. *Psychiatric Rehabilitation Journal, 32*(3), 215–222.

Husserl, E. (1907/1964). *The idea of phenomenology.* The Hague: Nijhoff.

Hutzel, K. E., & Kim, I. (2013). Situating an art-based action research study within social justice theories. *Archives of Design Research, 26*(2), 35–53.

Inglis, T. (1997). Empowerment and emancipation. *Adult Education Quarterly, 48*(1), 3–17.

Ingold, T. (2000). Making culture and weaving the world. In P. M. Graves-Brown (Ed.), *Matter, materiality and modern culture.* London and New York: Routledge.

Ingold, T. (2007). *Lines: A brief history.* London and New York: Routledge.

Irwin, R. L. (2004). A/r/tography: A metonymic métissage. In R. L. Irwin & A. de Cosson (Eds.), *A/r/tography: Rendering self through arts-based living inquiry,* (pp. 27–38). Vancouver, BC: Pacific Educational Press.

Irwin, R., & de Cosson, A. (2004). *A/R/Tography: Rendering self through arts-based living enquiry.* Vancouver, BC: Pacific Educational Press.

Irwin, R. L., & de Cosson, A. (Eds.). (2004). *A/r/tography: Rendering self through arts-based living inquiry.* Vancouver, BC: Pacific Educational Press.

Irwin, R., Beer, R., Springgay, S., Grauer, K., Xiong, G., & Bickel, B. (2006). The rhizomatic relations of A/r/togrpahy. *Studies in Art Education, 48*(1), 70–88.

Irwin, R. L., & Springgay, S. (2008). A/r/tography as practice-based research. In S. Springgay, R. L. Irwin, C. Leggo, & P. Gouzouasis (Eds.), *Being with A/r/tography* (pp. xix–xxxiii). Rotterdam, The Netherlands: Sense Publishers.

Irwin, R. L., & Springgay, S. (2008). A/r/tography as practice-based research. In M. Cahnmann-Taylor & R. Siegesmund (Eds.), *Arts-based research in education: Foundations for practice* (pp. 103–124). London: Routledge.

Ito, M., Gutiérrez, K., Livingstone, S., Penuel, B., Rhodes, J., Salen, K., … Watkins. C. (2013). *Connected learning: An agenda for research and design.* Irvine, CA: Digital Media and Learning Research Hub.

Jackson, A. Y., & Mazzei, L. A. (2011). *Thinking with theory in qualitative research: Using epistemological frameworks in the production of meaning.* London: Routledge.

Jamieson, H. V. (2008). Real time, virtual space, live theatre. In S. Brennan & S. Ballard (Eds.), *The aotearoa digital arts reader.* Auckland: Aotearoa Digital Arts and Clouds.

Jando, D., Sabia, R. F., & Daniel, N. (2008). *The circus: 1870–1950.* Köln, Germany: Taschen.

Järvinen, A. (2001). Quake® goes the environment: Game aesthetics and archaeologies. *Digital Creativity, 12*(2), 67–76.

Järvinen, A. (2010). *The state of social in social games.* Gamasutra: The art and business of making games. Retrieved June 20, 2014 from http://www.gamasutra.com/view/feature/134548/the_state_of_social_in_social_games.php

Jaycox, L. H., McCaffrey, D. F., Ocampo, B. W., Shelley, G. A., Blake, S. M., Peterson, D. J., … Kub, J. E. (2006). Challenges in the evaluation and implementation of school-based prevention and intervention programs on sensitive topics American. *Journal of Evaluation, 27*(3), 320–336.

Johnson, M. (1999). Communication in healthcare: A review of some key issues. *Journal of Research in Nursing, 4,* 18–30.

Johnson, C., & Thomas, H. W. (2012). Artists@Google. Retreived July 13, 2013 from www.questionbridge. com; http://www.questionbridge.com/blog/?tag=google-talk

John-Steiner, V. (2000). *Creative collaboration.* Oxford: Oxford University Press.

Jones, S., & Woglom, J. F. (2013). Graphica: Comics arts-based educational research. *Harvard Educational Review, 83*(1), 168–189.

Kahle, B., & Internet, A. (1998). *Archiving digital cultural artifacts: Organizing an agenda for action.* Berkley, CA: D-lib magazine July/August. Retrieved July 21, 2012 from http://www.dlib.org/dlib/july98/07lyman.html

Kang Song, Y. I., & Gammel, J. A. (2011). Ecological mural as community reconnection. *International Journal of Art & Design Education, 30,* 266–278.

Kay, L. (2013). Bead collage: An arts-based research method. *International Journal of Education and the Arts, 14*(3). Retrieved March 20, 2014 from http://www.ijea.org/v14n3/

Kayrouz, D. (2013). The use of art-based-initiatives for large sale organisational change: Case study. *Arts in Management: Special Issue, 8*(5), 56–66.

Kemmis, S., & McTaggart, R. (1988). *The action research planner*. Geelong, Victoria: Deakin University Press.

Kershaw, B., & Nicholson, H. (2011). *Research methods in theatre and performance*. Edinburgh: Edinburgh University Press.

Kerry-Moran, K. J. (2008). Between scholarship and art: Dramaturgy and quality in arts-related research. In J. G. Knowles & A. L. Cole (Eds.), *Handbook of education and the arts in qualitative research* (pp. 493–450). Thousand Oaks, CA: Sage.

Kidd, S. A., & Kral, M. J. (2005). Practicing participatory action research. *Journal of Counseling Psychology, 52*(2), 187–195.

Kim, O. (1999). Predictors of loneliness in elderly Korean immigrant women living in the United States of America. *Journal of Advanced Nursing, 29*(5), 1082–1088.

Kilroy, A., Garner, C., Parkinson C., Kagan, C., & Senior, P. (2007). *Towards transformation: Explaining the impact of culture, creativity and the arts on health and wellbeing*. Manchester: Manchester Metropolitan University.

Kirova, A., & Emme, M. (2006). Using photography as a means of phenomenological seeing: Doing phenomenology: With immigrant children. *Indo-Pacific Journal of Phenomenology Special Edition: Methods in Phenomenology, 6*, 1–12.

Knowles, J. G., & Cole, A. L. (2008). *Handbook of the arts in qualitative research*. London: Sage.

Ladkin, D., & Taylor, S. S. (2010). Enacting the 'true self': Towards a theory of embodied authentic leadership. *Leadership Quarterly, 21*, 64–74.

LaJevic, L., & Springgay, S. (2008). A/r/tography as an ethics of embodiment: Visual journals in pre-service education. *Qualitative Inquiry, 14*(1), 67–89.

Lawrence Lightfoot, S. (1983). *The good high school: Portraits of character and culture*. New York, NY: Basic Books.

Lea, G., Belliveau, G., Wager, A., & Beck, J. (2011). A loud silence: Working with research-based theatre and A/R/Tography. *International Journal of Education and the Arts, 12*(16), Retrieved July 03, 2014 from http://www.ijea.org/v12n16/

Leggo, C. (2008). Narrative inquiry: Attending to the art of discourse. *Language and Literacy, 10*(1), 21.

Leggo, C. (2010). Writing a life: Representation in language and image. *Transnational Curriculum Inquiry, 7*(2), 47–61.

Lemert, C. (2007). *Thinking the unthinkable: The riddles of classical social theories*. Boulder, CO: Paradigm Publishers.

Letherby, G., Brady, G. M., & Brown, G. C. (2007). Working with the community: Research and action. In C. J. Clay, M. Madden, & L. Potts (Eds.), *Towards understanding community: People and places*. Basingstoke: Palgrave Macmillan.

Levy, L., & Weber, S. (2011). Teenmom.ca: A community arts-based new media empowerment project for teenage mothers. *Studies in Art Education, 524*, 292–309

Liebman, D. (2009). Reflections on the artistic process. Retrieved June 17, 2014 from http://www.daveliebman.com/earticles2.php?DOC_INST=2

Liamputtong, P., & Rumbold, J. (2008). Knowing differently: Setting the scene. In P. Liamputtong & J. Rumbold (Eds.), *Knowing differently: Arts-based and collaborative research methods* (pp. 1–24). New York, NY: Nova Science Publishers, Inc.

Lincoln, Y. S., & Guba, E. G. (1985). *Naturalistic inquiry*. Newbury Park, CA: Sage.

Lincoln, Y., & Denzin, N. (2003). *Turning points in qualitative research: Tying knots in a handkerchief*. Walnut Creek, CA: Altamira Press.

Lister, M., Dovey, J., Giddings, S., Grant, I., & Kelly, K. (2009). *New media: A critical introduction* (2nd ed). London: Routledge.

Luanaigh, C. O., & Lawlor, B. A. (2008). Loneliness and the health of older people. *International Journal of Geriatric Psychiatry, 23*(12), 1213–1221.

Ludivine, A. F. (2009). *Practice-as-research: In performance and screen*. Basingstoke: Palgrave Macmillan.

REFERENCES

Lorenzo, T. (2010). Listening spaces: Connecting diverse voices for social action and change. In M. Savin-Baden & C. H. Major (Eds.), *New approaches to qualitative research: Wisdom & uncertainty* (pp. 131–143). London: Routledge.

Lowe, K. (2002). *What's the story? Making meaning in primary classrooms.* Sydney: Primary English Teaching Association.

Jones, K. (2006). A biographic researcher in pursuit of an aesthetic: The use of arts-based (re)presentations in 'performative' dissemination of life stories. *Qualitative Sociology Review, 2*(1), 66–85.

Jones, K. (2012). Connecting research with communities through performative social science. *The Qualitative Report, 17*(18), 1–8.

Macfarlane, B. (2010). Values and virtues in qualitative research. In M. Savin-Baden & C. H. Major (Eds.), *New approaches to qualitative research: Wisdom and uncertainty* (pp. 19–27). New York/ Abingdon: Routledge.

MacIntyre, A. (1990). *Three rival versions of moral enquiry.* London: Duckworth.

McIntyre, M. (2000). *Garden as phenomenon, method & metaphor in the context of health care: An arts informed life history* (Unpublished PhD Thesis). University of Toronto, Canada.

MacKenzie, S. K., & Wolf, M. M. (2012). Layering Sel(f)ves: Finding acceptance, community and praxis through collage. *The Qualitative Report, 17*(31), 1–21.

MacNaughton, J., White, M., & Stacey, R. (2005). Researching the benefits of arts in health. *Health Education, 105*(5), 332–339.

McGeoch, K.(2011). *Digital storytelling in second language learning and teaching* (Unpublished PhD). Sydney: University of Sydney.

McLuhan, M. (1964). *Understanding media: The extensions of man* (p. 7). Massachusetts, MA: First MIT Press.

McNiff, S. (1998). *Arts-based research.* London: Jessica Kingsley.

McNiff, S. (1998). *Trust the process: An artist's guide to letting go.* Boston: Shambala Publications.

McNiff, S. (2008). Arts-based research. In J. G. Knowles & A. L. Cole (Eds.), *Handbook of education and the arts in qualitative research* (pp. 29–40). Thousand Oaks, CA: Sage.

Major, C. H., & Savin-Baden, M. (2010a). *An introduction to qualitative research synthesis: Managing the information explosion in social science research.* London: Routledge.

Major, C. H., & Savin-Baden, M. (2010b). Exploring the relevance of qualitative research synthesis to higher education research and practice. *London Review of Education, 8*(2), 127–140.

Markus, P. (2007). *Drawing on experience* (Unpublished doctoral dissertation). McGill University, Montreal, QC.

Maxwell, J. A., & Miller, B. (2008). Categorizing and connecting strategies in qualitative data Analysis. In P. Leavy & S. Hesse-Biber (Eds.), *Handbook of emergent methods* (pp. 461–477). New York, NY: Guilford.

Mesher, P. (2006). *Documentation in an elementary classroom: A teacher-researcher study* (Unpublished doctoral dissertation). McGill University, Montreal, QC.

Merleau-Ponty, M. (1962). *Phenomenology of perception.* London and New York: Routledge and Kegan Paul.

Mezirow, J. (1981). A critical theory of adult learning and education. *Adult Education, 32*, 3–24.

Mezirow, J. (1991). *Transformative dimensions of adult learning.* San Francisco, CA: Jossey Bass.

Mezirow, J. (2000). *Learning as transformation: Critical perspectives on a theory in progress.* San Francisco, CA: Jossey Bass.

Moon, J. (2001). *PDP working paper 4 reflection in higher education learning.* York: Higher Education Academy. Retrieved July 15, 2014 from http://www.heacademy.ac.uk/resources/detail/resource_ database/id72_Reflection_in_Higher_Education_Learning

Morgan, T. (2013). Sharing, hacking, helping: Towards an understanding of digital aesthetics through a survey of digital art practices in Ireland. *Journal of Media Practice, 14*(2), 147–160.

Morrison, M., Davies, A., Brečević, G., Sem, I., Boykett, T., & Brečević, R. (2010). Designing performativity for mixed reality installations. *FORMakademisk, 3*(1), 123–144.

NHS Confederation. (2010). *From illness to wellness: Achieving efficiencies and improving outcomes.* London: Office of the Deputy Prime Minister. Retrieved March 08, 2012 from http://www.nhsconfed. org/Publications/Documents/illness_to_wellness_24 011.pdf

National Institute for Health and Clinical Excellence. (2008). *Mental wellbeing and older people*. London: Office of the Deputy Prime Minister. Retrieved March 09, 2012 from http://guidance.nice. org.uk/PH16

National Arts Policy Roundtable. (2011). *Innovating for Impact: Arts-based solutions for stronger America*. Retrieved March 08, 2012 from http://www.americansforthearts.org/information_services/ research/policy_roundtable/006.asp

Neilsen, L. (1998). *Knowing her place: Research literacies and feminist occasions*. San Francisco, CA: Caddo Gap Press/Backalong Books.

Nicholson, L. J. (1990). *Feminism/postmodernism*. London: Routledge.

Nightingale, D. J., & Cromby, J. (Eds.). (1999). *Social constructionist psychology: A critical analysis of theory and practice*. Buckingham: Open University Press.

Norris, J. (2000). Drama as research: Realising the potential of drama in education as a research methodology. *Youth Theatre Journal, 14*, 40–51.

O'Toole, J., & Beckett, D. (2010). *Educational research: Creative thinking and doing*. Oxford: Oxford University Press.

Palmar, I., & Nascimento, O. (2002). Health action theatre by seniors: Community development and education with groups of diverse languages and cultures. *Generations, 26*(3), 65–68.

Park-Fuller, L. (2000). Performing absence: The staged personal narrative as testimony. *Text and Performance Quarterly, 20*(1), 20–42.

Park-Fuller, L. (2003). A clean breast of it. In L. C. Miller, J. Taylor, & M. H. Carver (Eds.), *Voices made flesh: Performing women's autobiography* (pp. 215–236). Madison, WI: University of Wisconsin Press.

Parr, H. (2007). Collaborative film-making as process, method and text in mental health research. *Cultural Geographies, 14*(1), 114–138.

Piercy, F. P., McWey, L., Tice, S., James, E., Morris, M., & Arthur, K. (2005). It was the best of times, it was the worst of times: Doctoral students experiences of family research training through alternate forms of data representation. *Family Process, 44*(3), 363–378.

Pink, S. (2001). *Doing visual ethnography: Images, media and representation in research*. Thousand Oaks, CA: Sage Publications.

Piirto, J. (2002). The question of quality and qualifications: Writing inferior poems as qualitative research. *Qualitative Studies in Education, 15*(4), 431–445.

Polkinghorne, D. E. (1987). *Narrative knowing and the human sciences*. New York, NY: Suny Press.

Popper, K.R. (1970). Normal science and its dangers. In I. Lakatos & A. Musgrave (Eds.), *Criticisms and the growth of knowledge*. Cambridge: Cambridge University Press.

Putnam, R. D. (2000). *Bowling alone*. New York, NY: Free Press.

Rabkin, N., & Hedberg, E. (2011). *Arts education in America: What the declines mean for arts participation* (Research Report #52). Washington, DC: National Endowment for the Arts.

Reilly, M. (1962). Eleanor Clarke Slagle lecture: Occupational therapy can be one of the great ideas of 20th-century medicine. *American Journal of Occupational Therapy, 16*, 1–9.

Reingold, R. (2014). Moses' black wife: A case study analysis of secondary school students' arts-based projects. *Journal of Jewish Education, 80*(2), 99–120.

Respress, T., & Lutfi, G. (2006). Whole brain learning: The fine arts with students at risk. *Reclaiming Children & Youth, 15*(1), 24–31.

Rice, C. (2010). The space-time of pre-emption: An interview with Brian Massumi. *Architectural Design, 80*(5), 32–37.

Richardson, L. (2000). Introduction. Assessing alternative modes of qualitative and ethnographic research: How do we judge? Who judges? *Qualitative Inquiry, 6*(2), 251–255.

Riessman, C. K. (2008). *Narrative methods for the human sciences*. London: Sage

Rowe, N., Jones, C. H., Seeger, L., Greaves, G., Holman, C., & Turner, H. (2011). Forgetting the machine: Patients experiences of engaging in artwork while on renal dialysis. *Journal of Applied Arts and Health, 2*(1), 57–72

Richardson, L., & Lockridge, E. (1998). Fiction and ethnography: A conversation. *Qualitative Inquiry, 4*(3), 328–336.

Rogers, C. (1983). *Freedom to Learn for the 80's.* Columbus, Ohio: Merrill.

Rostan, S. M. (2010). Studio learning: Motivation, competence, and the development of young art students' talent and creativity. *Creativity Research Journal, 22,* 261–271.

Saldaña, J. (2005). *Ethnodrama: An anthology of reality theatre.* Walnut Creek, CA: AltaMira Press.

Saldaña, J. (2010). Writing ethnodrama: A sampler from educational research. In M. Savin-Baden & C. Major. *New approaches to qualitative research: Wisdom and uncertainty.* London: Routledge.

Salmon, P. (1989). Personal stances in learning. In S. Weil & I. McGill (Eds.), *Making sense of experiential learning.* Buckingham: Open University Press/SRHE.

Salmon, P., & Riessman, C. K. (2008). Looking back on narrative research: An exchange. In M. Andrews, C. Squire, & M. Tamboukou (Eds.), *Doing narrative research* (pp. 78–86). London: Routledge.

Savin-Baden, M. (2015). *Rethinking learning in an age of digital fluency: Is being digitally tethered a new learning nexus?* London: Routledge.

Savin-Baden, M., & Fisher, A. (2002). Negotiating 'honesties' in the research process. *British Journal of Occupational Therapy, 65*(4), 191–193.

Savin-Baden, M., & Major, C. (Eds.). (2012). *New approaches to qualitative research: Wisdom and uncertainty.* London: Routledge.

Savin-Baden, M., & Major, C. (2013). *Qualitative research: The essential guide to theory and practice.* London: Routledge.

Savin-Baden, M., Brady, G., Wimpenny, K., & Brown, G. (2013). *Evaluation of the Belgrade Theatre creative gymnasium project.* Report, Esmée Fairbairn, UK.

Schratz, M., & Walker, R. (1995). *Research as a social change: New opportunities for qualitative research.* London: Routledge.

Schwandt, T. A. (2001). *Dictionary of qualitative research.* Thousand Oaks, CA: Sage.

Seeley, C., & Reason, P. (2008). Expressions of energy: An epistemology of presentational knowing. In P. Liamputtong & J. Rumblod (Eds.), *Knowing differently: Arts based and collaborative research* (pp. 25–46). New York, NY: Nova Science Publishers, Inc.

Siegesmund, R., & Cahnmann-Taylor, M. (2008). Tensions of arts-based research reconsidered. In M. Cahnmann-Taylor & R. Siegesmund (Eds.), *Arts based research in education: Foundations for practice* (pp. 231–246). New York and London: Routledge.

Simons, H., & McCormack, B. (2007). Integrating arts-based inquiry in evaluation methodology: Opportunities and challenges. *Qualitative Inquiry, 13*(2), 292–311.

Sinclair, M. (2012). Artistic approaches to data collection: Illustrations and collage. *Evidence Based Midwifery, 10*(1), 3.

Sinding, C., Gray, R., & Nisker, J. (2008). Ethical issues and issues of ethics. In G. Knowles & A. Cole (Eds.), *Handbook of the arts in qualitative research* (pp. 459–467). London: Sage.

Sierz, A. (2010, February). Blasted and after: New writing in British Theatre today. Art workers' guild, 6 Queen's square, Bloomsbury, London. Retrieved February 20, 2010 from http://www.str.org.uk/events/lectures/archive/lecture1002.shtml

Skingley, A., & Vella-Burrows, T. (2010). Therapeutic effects of music and singing for older people. *Nursing Standard, 24*(19), 35–41.

Skingley, A., Clift, S. M., Coulton, S.P., & Rodriguez, J. (2011). The effectiveness and cost effectiveness of a participative community signing programme as a health promotion initiative for older people: Protocol for a randomized control trial. *BMC Public Health, 11,* 142.

Skwarek, M., & Pappenheimer, W. (2011, January). *Gradually melt the sky.* Retrieved July 13, 2013 from http://graduallymeltthesky.wordpress.com/

Slater, M. (2009). Place illusion and plausibility can lead to realistic behaviour in immersive virtual environments. *Philosophical Transactions of the Royal Society of London. Series B, Biological sciences, 364*(1535), 3549–3557.

Shutte, A. (1993). *Philosophy for Africa.* Cape Town: University of Cape Town Press.

Smith, D. (2002, November). *Arts-Informed inquiry: A new paradigm?* Key note address at Arts-Informed Inquiry Symposium. University of Sydney, Sydney.

Smith, H., Dean, R. T. (2009). Introduction: Practice-Led research. Research-Led Practice –Towards the iterative cyclic web. In H. Smith & R. T. Dean (Eds.), *Practice-Led research. Research-Led practice in the creative arts* (pp. 1–38). Edinburgh: Edinburgh University Press.

Sowbel, S. B. (2011). *Visual activity and relatedness: A portrait of ways the eye, empathy and ethics conjoin.* Ann Arbor, MI: ProQuest, UMI Dissertation Publishing.

Social Exclusion Unit. (2004). *Mental health and social exclusion: Social exclusion unit report.* London: Office of the Deputy Prime Minister. Retrieved March 08, 2012 from http://www.socialfirmsuk.co.uk/resources/library/mental-health-and-social-exclusion-social-exclusion-unit-report

Sousanis, N. (2013, April–May). *Thinking through comics: A doctoral dissertation in comics.* Spin Weave and Cut. Paper presented at AERA Annual Meeting and Exhibition, San Francisco, CA.

Springgay, S., Irwin, R. L., & Kind, S. (2008). A/r/tographers and living inquiry. In J. G. Knowles & A. L. Cole (Eds.), *Handbook of the arts in qualitative research: Perspectives, methodologies, examples, and issues* (pp. 83–91). Los Angeles, CA: SAGE Publications.

Springgay, S., Iriwn, R., & Kind, S. (2005). A/r/tography as living inquiry through art and text. *Qualitative Inquiry, 11*(6), 897–912.

Stacey, G., & Stickley, T. (2010). The meaning of art to people who use mental health services. *Perspectives in Public Health, 130*(2), 70–77.

Steeves, P. (2000). *Crazy quilt: Continuity, identity and a storied landscape in transition: A teacher's and a principal's work in progress* (Unpublished doctoral dissertation). University of Alberta, Edmonton, AB.

Stewart, R. (2008). Creating new stories for praxis: Navigations, narrations, neonarratives. In E. Barrett & B. Bolt (Eds.), *Practice as research: A guide* (pp. 123–134). London/New York: I.B Tauris.

Stogner, M. (2014). Two sides of the same stone. *The International Journal of New Media, Technology and the Arts, 8*(1), 11–21.

Stogner, M. (2013, June). *Searching for aristotle in the digital age: Creating cultural narrative with 21st century media.* Paper presented at the 8th International Conference of Arts in Society, Budapest, Hungary. Retrieved from http://www.bluebearfilms.com/2013/maggie-burnette-stogner-at-the-international-conference-on-arts-in-society/ Technologies

Stogner, M. B. (2009). Searching for aristotle in the digital age: Creating cultural narrative with 21st century media technologies. The media-enhanced museum experience. *Curator, 54*:4.

Stronach, I., Corbin, B., Mcnamara, O., Stark, S., & Warne, T. (2002). Towards an uncertain politics of professionalism: Teacher and nurse identities in flux. *Journal of Educational Policy, 17*(1), 109–138.

Sullivan, G. (2004). *Art practice as research: Inquiry in the visual arts.* Thousand Oaks, CA: Sage.

Sullivan, G. (2006). Research acts in practice. *Studies in Art Education, 48*(1), 19–35.

Sullivan, G. (2009). Making space: The purpose and place of practice led research. In H. Smith & R. T. Dean (Eds.), *Practice-Led research. Research-Led practice in the creative arts* (pp. 41–65). Edinburgh: Edinburgh University Press.

Sullivan, A. (2009). Defining poetic occasion in inquiry: Concreteness, voice, ambiguity, tension, and associative logic. In M. Prendergast (Ed.), *Poetic inquiry: Vibrant voices in the social sciences* (pp. 111–126). Rotterdam: Sense.

Sullivan, G. (2010). *Art practice as research: Inquiry in the visual arts* (2nd ed). London: Sage.

Suppes, P., Esiner, E., Stanley, J., & Grenne, M. (1998). The vision thing: Educational research and AERA in the 21st Century – Part 5: A vision for Educational Research and AERA in the 12st Century. *Educational Researcher, 27*(9), 33–35.

Sutherland, I. (2013). Arts-based methods in leadership development: Affording aesthetic workspaces, reflexivity and memory with momentum. *Management Learning, 44*(1), 25–43.

Sviden, G., Tham, K., & Borell, L. (2004). Elderly participants of social and rehabilitative centers. *Scandinavian Journal of Caring Science, 18*(4), 402–409.

Stake, R. (1995). *The art of case research.* Thousand Oaks, CA: Sage.

Taylor, S. S., & Ladkin, D. (2009). Understanding arts-based methods in managerial development. *Academy of Management Learning and Education, 8*(1), 55–69.

Tennant, R., Hiller, L., Fishwick, R. Platt, S., Joseph, S., Weich, S., . . . Stewart-Brown, S. (2007). *Warwick-Edinburgh Mental Well-Being Scale* (WEMWBS). Retrieved Novemeber 28, 2012 from http://www.hqlo.com/content/5/1/63

Tett, L., Anderson, K., McNeill, F., Overy, K., & Sparks, R. (2012). Learning, rehabilitation and the arts in prisons: A Scottish case. *Study Studies in the Education of Adults, 44*(2), 171–185.

Townsend, E. (1996). Institutional ethnography: A method for analysing practice. *Occupational Therapy Journal of Research. 16*(3), 179–199.

Trowler, P. (2013). Can approaches to research in art and design be beneficially adapted for research into higher education? *Higher Education Research and Development, 32*(1), 56–69.

Turk, T. (2010). Your own imagination: Vidding and vidwatching as collaborative interpretation. *Film and Film Culture, 5*, 88–110.

Ulmer, G. (1985). *Applied grammatology: Post(e)-Pedagogy from Jacques Derrida to Joseph Beuys.* Baltimore, MD: Johns Hopkins University Press.

Upton, I. (2012). *Extract/insert.* Retrieved July 15, 2014 from http://www.get-real-solutions.co.uk

Wang, C., & Burris, M. A. (1994). Empowerment through photo novella: Portraits of participation. *Health Education and Behavior, 21*(2), 171–186.

Watson, R., & Fourie, M. (2004). Occupation and occupational therapy. In R. Watson & L. Swartz (Eds.), *Transformation through occupation* (pp. 19–32). London, PA: Whurr Publishers.

Weaver-Hightower, M. B. (2010). Assessing the uses of sequential art for qualitative research. Paper presented at the American Educational Research Association, Denver, CO.

Weinstein, S. (2010). A unified poet alliance: The personal and social outcomes of youth spoken word poetry programming. *International Journal of Education & the Arts, 11*(2). Retrieved July 14, 2014 from http://www.ijea.org/v11n2/

Wengraf, T. (2001). *Qualitative research interviewing: Biographic narrative and semi-structured method.* London: Sage.

White, B. (2013). *Aesthetics, empathy and education: Poetry as empathic response to personal, intellectual and moral poverty.* Paper presented at the American Educational Research Association (AERA), San Francisco, CA.

White, V., & Belliveau, G. (2010). Whose story is it anyway? Exploring ethical dilemmas in performed research. *Performing Ethos International Research Journal, 1*(1), 85–95.

White, V., & Belliveau, G. (2011). Multiple perspectives, loyalties and identities: Exploring intrapersonal spaces through research-based theatre. *International Journal of Qualitative Studies in Education, 24*(2), 227–238.

White, M., & Angus, J. (2003). *Arts and adult mental health literature review.* Durham: University of Durham (CAHHM).

Whittemore, R., Chase, S. K., & Mandle, C. L. (2001). Validity in qualitative research. *Qualitative Health Research, 11*, 522–537.

Wilson, S. (1996). *Myths and confusions in thinking about Art/Science/Technology: Art as research.* Paper presented at College Art Association Meetings, NYC, 2000. Retrieved July 09, 2014 from http://userwww.sfsu.edu/swilson/papers/artist.researcher.html

Wimpenny, K., & Savin-Baden, M. (2014). Using theatre and performance for promoting health and well being amongst the 50+ community: An arts-informed evaluation. *The International Journal of Social, Political, and Community Agendas in the Arts, 8*(1), 47–64.

Wood, L., Ivery, P., Donovan, R., & Lambin, E. (2013). To the beat of a different drum: improving the social and mental well being of at-risk young people through drumming. *Journal of Public Mental Health, 12*(2), 70–79.

Woolf, V. (1940). *Orlando.* Florida, FL: Harcourt Brace Jovanaovich.

Wright, R., John, L., Alaggia, R., & Sheel, J. (2006). Community-based arts program for youth in low-income communities: A multi-method evaluation. *Child and Adolescent Social Work Journal, 23*, 635–652.

Yin, R. K. (1984). *Case study research: Design and methods* (1st ed). Beverly Hills, CA: Sage.

# INDEX

Lightning Source UK Ltd.
Milton Keynes UK
UKOW07f1358050115

244019UK00007B/556/P